# The Girl's Guide To Relationships, Sexuality & Consent

## Tools To Help Teens Stay Safe, Empowered & Confident

Leah Aguirre, LCSW
Geraldine O'Sullivan, LCSW

16pt

# Copyright Page from the Original Book

### Publisher's Note

*This book is presented solely for educational purposes. The authors and publisher are not offering it as legal, therapeutic, or other professional services; they assume no liabilities with respect to the accuracy or completeness of the contents. Neither the authors nor the publisher shall be held liable or responsible to any person or entity with respect to any loss or any damages caused or alleged to have been caused, directly or not, by the information or programs contained herein. No warranty may be created or extended by sales representatives or written sales materials. This book is not designed to substitute psychological, financial, legal, or other professional services, and you should seek the services of a competent professional before making significant changes or life decisions.*

*While this book reflects common situations and experiences, the characters, entities, names, and stories are purely fictional. Any likeness to actual people, either living or dead, is strictly coincidental.*

INSTANT HELP, the Clock Logo, and NEW HARBINGER are trademarks of New Harbinger Publications, Inc.

New Harbinger Publications is an employee-owned company.

Copyright © 2022 by Leah Aguirre and Geraldine O'Sullivan
          Instant Help Books
          An imprint of New Harbinger Publications, Inc.
          5674 Shattuck Avenue
          Oakland, CA 94609
          www.newharbinger.com

All Rights Reserved

Cover design by Amy Shoup; Acquired by Georgia Kolias; Edited by Teja Watson

---

### Library of Congress Cataloging-in-Publication Data

Names: Aguirre, Leah, author. | O'Sullivan, Geraldine, author.
Title: The girl's guide to relationships, sexuality, and consent : tools to help teens stay safe, empowered, and confident / Leah Aguirre, Geraldine O'Sullivan.
Description: Oakland, CA : Instant Help Books, [2022] | Series: The instant help solutions series | Includes bibliographical references.
Subjects: LCSH: Teenage girls--Conduct of life--Juvenile literature. | Dating (Social customs)--Juvenile literature. | Sexual ethics for teenagers--Juvenile literature. | Interpersonal relations in adolescence--Juvenile literature. | BISAC: YOUNG ADULT NONFICTION / Social Topics / Dating & Sex | YOUNG ADULT NONFICTION / Social Topics / Self-Esteem & Self-Reliance
Classification: LCC HQ798 .A49 2022 | DDC 305.235/2--dc23/eng/20220425
LC record available at https://lccn.loc.gov/2022018697

# TABLE OF CONTENTS

| | |
|---|---|
| A Note for Caring Adults | vi |
| Welcome | viii |
| CHAPTER 1: So, What's Important to You? | 1 |
| CHAPTER 2: Know Your Worth and Others Will Too | 20 |
| CHAPTER 3: Sexual "I"dentity Celebrates Who You Are | 36 |
| CHAPTER 4: Your Own Body Love Comes First | 53 |
| CHAPTER 5: Choosing Your Circle of Friends | 73 |
| CHAPTER 6: Loving When It's Healthy and Knowing When It's Not | 94 |
| CHAPTER 7: Online Love Doesn't Feel Virtual | 118 |
| CHAPTER 8: Sex, No Sex, or Something Else? Set Your Terms | 138 |
| CHAPTER 9: Staying Safe During Sex | 161 |
| CHAPTER 10: Breakups Are Tough—but So Are You | 178 |
| CHAPTER 11: Some News About Sexting and Nudes | 203 |
| PARTING GIFT: Your Decisions Are the Power in Sexual Empowerment | 219 |
| Acknowledgments | 223 |
| Resources | 225 |
| References | 234 |
| Back Cover Material | 238 |

"Teenaged girls today face many challenges, but they hesitate to initiate potentially awkward conversations with the adults in their lives. Often, they don't know enough about their concerns to figure out what information or guidance they need, or how to get it. *The Girl's Guide to Relationships, Sexuality, and Consent* precisely provides the content, support, wisdom, accessibility, and privacy girls want and need. Thank you, Leah and Geraldine!"

—**Debra Gilbert Rosenberg, AM, LCSW**, psychotherapist for more than thirty-five years, and author of *The New Moms' Companion* and *Motherhood without Guilt*

"As a psychologist specializing in teen girls, I will certainly have this book prominently displayed in my office! It educates and clarifies one of the most timely and sensitive topics facing teens today. I am grateful to the authors for covering this massive topic so comprehensively, and in a way that leaves the reader with a greater sense of agency and empowerment. It's a must-have resource for every teen."

—**Lucie Hemmen, PhD**, clinical psychologist, and author of *Parenting a Teen Girl*

"I wish I'd had this sex-positive, psychologically astute, nonjudgmental, kind, and inclusive guide when I was a teenager! Actually, it probably would have helped me in my twenties as well. This book respects the intelligence of young people to work through complex questions of desire, consent, and safety. A great gift for your daughter, niece, or any other young people in your life."

—**Rachel Krantz,** award-winning journalist, and author of *Open*

"Leah and Geraldine have created an outstanding resource on a sensitive and significant topic. This book is a comprehensive and straightforward guide to all aspects of dating, from building self-esteem to navigating breakups to the legal and emotional ramifications of sex without consent. With the pervasive internet component in today's social environment, teaching teens to stay physically and emotionally healthy in dating relationships is critical. Teen boys should read this, too!"

—**Lisa M. Schab, LCSW,** psychotherapist; and author of eighteen self-help books, including *The Self-Esteem Workbook for Teens* and the *Put Your Worries Here* journaling series

"*The Girl's Guide to Relationships, Sexuality, and Consent* has the guidance, language, and specific tools for teens to explore some of the most challenging parts of navigating this period of their lives. Brilliantly written and with examples that are relatable and easy to read, teens and their parents will benefit greatly from this resource!"

—**Jessica Yaffa, CPC,** certified professional relationship coach, and president of NoSilence NoViolence

"I am wholeheartedly recommending this book to my patients! A very thoughtful and inclusive resource, written by experienced therapists, to help teens and their families navigate the complex and challenging topics of relationships, identity formation, and much more!"
—**Kali Hobson, MD,** adult, child, and adolescent psychiatrist

## the instant help solutions series

Young people today need mental health resources more than ever. That's why New Harbinger created the **Instant Help Solutions Series** especially for teens. Written by leading psychologists, physicians, and professionals, these evidence-based self-help books offer practical tips and strategies for dealing with a variety of mental health issues and life challenges teens face, such as depression, anxiety, bullying, eating disorders, trauma, and self-esteem problems.

Studies have shown that young people who learn healthy coping skills early on are better able to navigate problems later in life. Engaging and easy-to-use, these books provide teens with the tools they need to thrive—at home, at school, and on into adulthood.

This series is part of the **New Harbinger Instant Help Books** imprint, founded by renowned child psychologist Lawrence Shapiro. For a complete list of books in this series, visit newharbinger.com.

*For my mom and dad, both social workers, for instilling the values and beliefs that have made me the person I am today and inspired me to do the work I do.* —Leah Aguirre

*For my dad, who married a strong, educated woman and raised three strong, educated women. Thank you for leading by example in the value of respecting women.* —Geraldine O'Sullivan

# A Note for Caring Adults

To the parents, caregivers, and compassionate adults who have chosen this book for their teen, we thank you! It can be challenging to navigate complex and sensitive conversations with your teen about relationships, sexuality, self-esteem, and identity. By selecting this book for your teen, you've taken a great step in helping her to develop a healthy understanding of who she is and how she fits into the world we live in today.

As therapists, we are familiar with the difficulties girls face in today's environment, especially within the digital culture of social media. Whether it be unrealistic expectations of physical appearance, pressure to send/receive explicit images, physical or online harassment, or unhealthy relationships, these challenges can take a toll on mental health and self-worth.

To combat them, our priority is to empower girls to identify their values and enhance their self-esteem. We believe that this lays the groundwork for healthy relationship choices. Educating teens about sexuality helps to build confidence, prevent dating violence, and promote safe choices. Throughout the book, girls will learn to navigate relationships, breakups, and decision-making regarding sexual health. They'll also be provided with therapeutic exercises they can use to help them along the way.

We understand the natural concerns that caring adults may have when it comes to their teen's sexual development. Rest assured that this book serves to empower girls to make healthy, safe, and conscious choices based on their personal values. Throughout the book, readers are encouraged to have open and honest communication with trusted adults as they face new situations and challenges. We thank you for providing your teen with the opportunity to do that!

—Leah and Geraldine

# Welcome

Welcome! We are so happy you're here, starting this journey toward knowledge and empowerment. Being a teenager is an exciting time, during which you get to learn so much about yourself. It can also be challenging as you navigate the world around you, especially when it comes to the pressures of social media, sex, and all the other stuff that comes with growing up.

You aren't a kid, and you aren't yet an adult. As a teen, you are figuring out who you are, what you like, and what is important to you. You might be curious, seeking new experiences, and trying to express yourself in different ways. There's probably *a lot* going on—and it's completely normal to feel overwhelmed, nervous, and maybe sometimes insecure as you deal with it all. Whether you are going through a bad breakup, feeling betrayed by a friend, deciding when you're ready to have sex, or just trying to feel confident in your own skin, we're here to help! The fact that you are here and seeking some guidance tells us you want to feel empowered to become that strong, confident, and assertive person you are meant to be.

With that being said, we wrote this book for *you*. We are licensed clinical social workers who have spent years providing therapy to teens just like you. While we may not be in high school or in our teens anymore, we've been where you are, and we know the kinds of things you're going through. We also know that there are many girls who sometimes feel "not good enough" and struggle with their self-esteem. Throughout the book you'll notice that gendered terms like "girl" are used and we recognize that these terms do not reflect all identities. Know that we've written this book to honor and incorporate all identities including trans and non-binary teens.

We want you to know that you are not alone: so many other teens have been through the same things that you may be experiencing right now. We believe in the importance of being proactive and taking charge of the decisions that impact our mental and physical health, and we want the same for you.

Being empowered means having the ability to make choices and decisions that feel good and right for *you*. It also means feeling confident enough to express those choices and decisions to others, even when it's difficult. As you develop your identity and values, you will learn what it means to have a healthy relationship with yourself and others. You'll be able to assert yourself and feel comfortable communicating your needs, no matter what.

So many girls don't feel like they have a voice, or like their needs matter—especially when it comes to relationships and sex. Girls everywhere are affected by issues like unhealthy relationships with peers or romantic partners, judgment and shame for their sexuality—and even intense issues like sexual assault. Throughout this book, you'll read about a variety of scenarios and situations that you might be able to relate to, and you'll work through exercises that will help guide you in getting to know yourself, making the decisions you might need to make about your relationships, and having important conversations with people like friends, romantic partners, and the adults you trust about your decisions and your rights. We encourage you to grab a piece of paper or your favorite journal and keep it nearby for these exercises, and we hope you enjoy the time reflecting and practicing your new skills.

As you read through this book, you'll gain an understanding of who you are, what you want, and how to express it. You'll gain a new knowledge of yourself and what's important to you, skills to improve your self-esteem and body image, and an understanding of what a healthy relationship looks like.

We look forward to going on this journey with you, and we're here for you every step of the way!

With love,
Leah and Geraldine

# CHAPTER I

# So, What's Important to You?

Becoming an adult is an exciting time, one of change, growth, and self-discovery. At this age, you start to see yourself as an individual—not just a child, sibling, or friend. You might be questioning the opinions or beliefs of your parents and family. You might pursue new interests and hobbies that are different from your friends' or the people around you. This is a time of curiosity and exploration, when you can envision your future and identify your own goals.

As you do this, you might be exploring new friendships and relationships, and maybe growing apart from some of your old friends. Or you might be dealing with tough stuff you've never dealt with before: dating, sex and intimacy, and other big life decisions that reflect what really matters to us in life.

While all these changes can be very exciting, you may also notice yourself feeling sad or down, or dealing with tough situations and questions that you've maybe never dealt with before. And that's okay! Change can be difficult, especially when you're going outside your comfort zone to try new things.

Through these explorations and new experiences, you also might start questioning some of the things that were important and meaningful to you in the past, and forming new beliefs and priorities. Being clear in your values—the things that matter most to you—can help guide decisions, form relationships, motivate you, and help you determine how you want to live your life.

In this chapter, we'll help you clarify what is most important to you. There are many different kinds of values. Your values could include:

Family
Spirituality
Education
Creativity
Adventure
Communication
Honesty
Giving Back to Community
Social Justice
Strength
Open-Mindedness
Respect

The list goes on! What's cool about values is that they're special and unique to you. We are all entitled to our own values and beliefs. And they can change as you change—as you get older and learn more about what you do and don't want. In fact, your values likely will change over the course of your life, as you go through all kinds of experiences—just as your identity changes and shifts. This is normal and part of your life journey.

In this chapter, we'll encourage you to think about your values and do some self-reflection. What is important to *you*? If you don't have a clue about what your personal values are, that's okay! That's why we're here, to guide you and help you learn more about yourself—which takes time.

First, let's look at how clarifying your values can be helpful—especially as your circle of friends and acquaintances might be growing and changing.

## When Your Values Differ From Your Friends' Values

When you were a kid, your values were often influenced and determined by your environment, whether through the teaching and behavior of your parents or caregivers, religion, school, media, and social interactions. However, as you evolve as a person and enter adulthood, you will start to think more independently and critically. You will begin to question some of the things that make you feel uncomfortable, or don't make sense to you anymore.

Consider what happens when your friends are doing things that, deep down, you don't want to do. Ask yourself, "Is this my value or someone else's?"

You will develop your own opinions and perspectives, which may challenge the opinions and perspectives of other people. While this can feel confusing and difficult, we want to help you see it as also beautiful and empowering.

Let's take a look at Genevieve's experience to see how she handles conflicting values.

*Genevieve is a sophomore. She gets good grades, plays soccer, and is part of her school's student government. Genevieve has always been a hard worker and values doing well on her schoolwork and academics. She already knows which college she wants to attend, and she wants to become a veterinarian. She is excited about this future, so she's prioritizing her academic and career goals.*

*Lately, two of her close friends have been ditching school during their fourth period class. Genevieve's seen their stories on social media and sometimes feels jealous that she isn't with them. They keep inviting her to cut class too, and sometimes her FOMO makes the idea feel tempting. But deep down, she doesn't know if it's worth it.*

*She's conflicted. Would it be terrible to ditch? Even if it was just one time?*

Genevieve is thinking about cutting class only because her friends are inviting her, and she doesn't want to feel left out anymore. She may be worried that she and her friends will start drifting apart if she doesn't join them, or that they'll start to think she's too boring.

Like Genevieve, your values and priorities can start to shift and become different than those of your friends'. This will happen at different stages throughout your life. As you start to think about your future, visualizing what you want your life to be or look like, you'll naturally start to spend more time doing the things that matter most to you ... and less time on things that aren't as important.

This can be really exciting! But sometimes you may resist changing, because you worry about losing friendships or losing closeness with friends. You may grieve how things used to be even as you grow into the person you want to be. This can feel really hard.

Social media doesn't help. Being aware of what everyone else is doing, all the time, can make it really hard to stick to your values and do what feels good for *you*. It's easy to compare yourself to others and feel pressured to do things just for the sake of fitting in or being liked. So, even if you are fully aware of your values and what's important to you, it can sometimes be difficult to honor those values when there's outside pressure.

Having differences in values is not necessarily a bad thing. It doesn't mean that one person's wrong and another person's right, or that one person is better than the other. And it's possible for friends to have differences in opinions or beliefs. What is most important is that you respect others' values and differences, and that they respect yours.

So, what are Genevieve's options? She could take some time to reflect on her values and personal goals—whether on her own or with a therapist or adult that she respects and looks up to. By clarifying her values and considering her future plans, she'd probably come to the realization that ditching class wouldn't be that helpful in the long term and could even hurt her. While it still may be difficult to see her friends hanging out without her, she'll feel more confident when she decides to stay at school.

Consider this: If these friends are *real* friends, they will respect Genevieve's decisions and choices. Even if they might give her a hard time here and there, they'll understand that school is a priority for her and let her do her thing. They will support her goals and aspirations, even if they differ from their own. On the other hand, if these friends were to make fun of Genevieve or start distancing themselves from her because of their differences in values, Genevieve might consider it a sign to start investing time in other relationships or friendships that are more encouraging. She might even try to build new friendships with people who are like-minded and share similar values.

Think ahead: What can you do if you think that some of your values conflict with your friends'? You could start by taking the time to reflect on and explore your values, so you can understand what they really are. You could remind yourself of your goals and how you envision your future. If you determine that your values differ from those of your friends or the people close to you, remember that it's okay. Your values are for you to choose and honor. And growing apart from people is a part of life.

See how important having clear values can be? Now it's your turn. This exercise can help you begin to learn more about yourself and your personal values.

## EXERCISE: GETTING CLEAR ABOUT YOUR VALUES

1. Grab your journal or piece of paper and write down 5–10 personal values. Remember, these are *your* values, the things that are important to *you*. If you need ideas, you can refer to the list at the start of the chapter, or check out the link in the resource section in the back of the book.
2. For each value, reflect and write down why this value is important to you.

    *Example:* If you value music, you might appreciate how it brings people together or how it can be a form of self-expression.

    *Example:* If you value family, you might appreciate spending time or sharing experiences with the people closest to you.

*Example:* If you value sports, you might appreciate how you can challenge yourself to become stronger and more skilled, or enjoy being on a team.

3. Pay attention to the thoughts and feelings that come up as you do this exercise.
   - Do you feel excited? Or frustrated that you aren't devoting more time to the things you value?
   - Is it easy to come up with things you care about, or difficult?
   - Do you worry that someone you love wouldn't approve of the values you wanted to pick?
   - You might recognize you need more time to think about this. If so, as you go through your day, keep the question in the back of your mind: *What is most important to me?*

Remember, your values can and will change. So, honor the need to take some time to explore what your values are. And know that what you came up with isn't set in stone. It'll change as you change.

## Do Your Values Clash?

As you begin to become more familiar with your values, you will notice that some of them contradict one another. This is part of becoming your own person—learning how to navigate and respond to values that don't always fit together nicely. You might end up reassessing your values or prioritizing one over another. Although this can be uncomfortable, it's a sign of growth and maturity. Remember, life is complex! Try to embrace being open to changes and shifts in your beliefs.

Let's take a look at what happened for Sammi when her values clashed with each other.

*Sammi values being social. She is outgoing and considered "popular" at school, but it's important to her to socialize with everyone and have friends in different groups.*

*Recently, her main friend group has been making fun of one of their classmates, Emilee. They make fun of her because she dresses "different." They call her names and make fun of how she looks—and occasionally Sammi joins in. She feels bad about it.*

*Still ... Sammi loves her friends and has known them since middle school. They helped cheer her up after a recent breakup and have ALWAYS been there for her. She doesn't think they are "bad" people, but she also doesn't like how they talk about Emilee and blast her over text and social media.*

Sammi has conflicting values; her values of friendship and being part of this group are at odds with her value of treating people with kindness, dignity, and respect. Although Sammi feels uncomfortable with her friends' behavior, she doesn't say anything to them and even joins in on the conversation.

As we get older and start to become more aware of who we are and what matters to us, it's common to start feeling uncomfortable when we do things that don't align with our values and beliefs. This is called "cognitive dissonance."

Cognitive dissonance is that feeling of discomfort you experience when you are acting or behaving in a way that is not aligned with who you are at your core. Sometimes this uncomfortable feeling shows up as tension in your body or tightness in your chest. You can think of this as your body signaling to you, "Hey, this doesn't seem like something you would do!" or "Are you sure you're comfortable with this?"

When you experience cognitive dissonance, it's a cue to pause and really think about the situation. Ask yourself:
1. Why am I feeling uncomfortable?
2. Is this situation going against my values and what I believe in?
3. What actions or decisions can I make that will better reflect my values and reduce this discomfort?

While this seems straightforward enough, it can be hard to do "the right thing" or make a decision that reflects your values when it requires you to challenge the actions of your friends or to go against mainstream culture. Human brains are wired to be social and seek connection with others. It's in our nature to want to fit in and be part of a larger group, because belonging to a group makes us feel safe and protected. Even if you are completely aware of and confident in your values, it's also normal to hesitate about speaking up—because you may also value being accepted. This is why so many teens struggle with peer pressure.

So, what can Sammi do? She has a few options. First, Sammi could decide that she will no longer participate in any conversations that involve gossiping or putting other people down. Just because her friends are making fun of someone, that doesn't mean she has to take part in it.

She could also try to talk to her friends and share her stance on the matter—maybe they will be open to her perspective and reflect on their own values and actions.

Sammi might also start to recognize that she may be outgrowing this group of friends, if they have few values in common or they don't accept her for who she is and what she stands for. While this may feel hard and sad, sometimes dilemmas such as this one offer an important learning experience. They help you grow as an individual—because you are willing to reevaluate and clarify your values.

What can you do if you're confronted with a similar situation? First, check in with your body and notice any tension or discomfort. Then pause and reflect on your personal values. Are they conflicting? If so, reevaluate some of the values you are questioning. Remember, it's okay if your values change or are different from those of your friends.

Sometimes, taking action is difficult or can feel intimidating. This next exercise will help you plan how you can start prioritizing your values—deciding which ones matter most to you and why, which is the first step in putting them into practice. It's okay to start small!

## EXERCISE: PRIORITIZE AND HONOR YOUR VALUES

It's important to prioritize and honor your values. When you are being true to yourself, you'll feel more confident in your relationships, decisions, and in pursuing your goals.

Using the values identified in the previous exercise, let's make a plan to incorporate at least two of them into your everyday life and routine.
- Identify the value you would like to reinforce/honor.
    Example: Kindness
- Identify a simple activity that would reflect this value.
    Example: I will offer help to those around me.
- Set a goal.
    Example: I will offer to help someone (friend, family member, classmate) at least once every day.

- Check in with yourself by asking the following questions:

    How do I feel when I am honoring my values consistently?
    Do I feel more confident?
    Do I feel more comfortable in my skin?
    What positive changes have I noticed since I started honoring my values more?

By giving yourself this time and space to think, you will be better prepared to act and make decisions that reflect who you are and what you believe in. While it can be difficult and uncomfortable to act in a way that's different than your friends (like putting your phone away to go sleep while the rest of your friends are messaging in a group chat), when you make choices that reflect your personal values you will feel more confident and at peace, because you are showing up as your authentic self. And who doesn't want that?

# Know What You Value in a Relationship

As you date and pursue relationships, you'll quickly learn that some of your values are specific to relationships and reflect what you want in a partner. Often, we tend to focus on things like attractiveness, sense of humor, and popularity, but there is so much more to consider! Some of these values could include trust, honesty, dependability, motivation, silliness, communication, physical affection—and so many more. When you're aware of what's most important to you in a relationship, you'll be better able to communicate your needs, set limits, and determine if a relationship is right for you.

If you aren't quite sure what you value in a relationship yet, that's okay. Now is the time to explore these values and preferences.

## EXERCISE: ADDING VALUES TO YOUR DATING "CHECKLIST"

As you think about the qualities you look for and want in a partner, also ask yourself what you value in a relationship. For example, you might value shared interests, spending time together, honesty, and respect. Take a moment to write a checklist, and include your values.

Example checklist:
- ☐ Athletic
- ☐ Listens to me and really gets me
- ☐ Likes my friends
- ☐ Good communicator
- ☐ Trustworthy
- ☐ Funny

Save this list for a rainy day, to refer back to and remind yourself of what you are looking for and deserve in a partner.

Now, let's take a look at Nadia's experience, as she explores her values in her relationship with her boyfriend, David.

*Nadia started dating David a couple months ago; this is her first real relationship. Lately she's been noticing that David has been taking a while to respond to her texts—sometimes it's hours, other times it can be a whole day. Nadia likes David, but because they go to different schools, they don't see each other often. When they are hanging out, everything is fine; they have fun and Nadia feels like David "gets" her. But when he takes so long to get back to her, she feels like he isn't really trying or doesn't care as much as she does. She wonders if she should break up with him, or if she's being too dramatic.*

What's happening with Nadia happens often. While she's aware of her values, she is also questioning them and struggling to figure out how they should align with those of her partner. In relationships, it's not uncommon to doubt yourself or your values—especially when you have strong feelings for your partner and want it to work out. But your values and what you want in a relationship are important.

So how can Nadia navigate this? Nadia could express or communicate her feelings to David. She could tell him that she values communication, that she isn't always feeling heard the way they're communicating now, and that maybe they can decide together what works for both of them in terms of how often they talk. This is different from her trying to control him and needing to be able to reach him at all times, or saying nothing and continuing to feel lonely and insecure in the relationship.

Nadia could also take some time to reflect on her values and what she wants in a relationship, perhaps write them down or talk it out with a friend. By grounding herself in her values, she will feel more confident when it's time to express them to David. And then, if it turns out that David can respect this value, great! But if he's resistant or unwilling to meet somewhere in the middle, maybe he's not the guy for her.

If you are in a similar situation and are feeling insecure or uncertain about a relationship, what do you do? We suggest checking in with yourself. Consider whether you're seeing the situation you're in accurately. Then ask yourself (honestly) what's important to you—what are the qualities that you want in a partner, and what do you value in a relationship? You might have the urge to change your list to make it fit your current situation or relationship, but try to stay true to yourself and communicate your values to your partner as they truly are.

And if there's any pushback from your partner, remember that you are entitled to your values, and that in a healthy relationship your values will be honored and respected by your partner.

## EXERCISE: COMMUNICATING YOUR VALUES TO YOUR PARTNER

Expressing your values and what is important to you can sometimes be uncomfortable, especially to someone new or someone you really like. Often people will hide their true feelings, thoughts, and opinions because they worry that their partner or the person they're dating won't agree or understand. But remember: You are entitled to your values. And your partner won't know how to respect them if it's not communicated to them.

When you are communicating your values to others, be clear and direct—you don't have to give a long-winded explanation. Here are some examples of statements that communicate values and needs:

> I care a lot about my friendships, and I want to make more time for my friends.
>
> I need to make more time for school—preparing for college is my priority right now.
>
> I care about you, and trust is really important. I need you to be able to trust me more, instead of questioning where I am or who I'm with.

Even though you're busy, communication is important to me, and I'd like to talk on the phone more often.

Now try forming your own statement. You can use this sentence structure as a guide.

_____ is important to me and I need _____.

I need _____ because I care about _____.

Learning how to communicate effectively requires practice—communication is a skill! Throughout this book, we will offer more opportunities to fine-tune your communication skills. It may feel awkward and unnatural at first, but with time you'll feel more and more confident—in order to be able to initiate and have these tougher conversations.

## Let's Recap: Values

As you begin this empowering journey of self-discovery and asserting yourself in relationships, remember to start with your values.

**Know Your Values:** Values are things that are important to us. They might be shaped by what our parents teach us, our culture, our religion, social media, society, our friends, or what our gut tells us! Every person has their own unique set of values—and once you figure out what yours are, you'll feel more confident in your ability to make a decision that's right for you.

**Know How to Deal with Value Conflicts:** Sometimes your own values may conflict with one another, which may require you to reevaluate them. This can be tricky but is important to learn how to do, as you get to know yourself.

**Understand Your Relationship Values:** Relationship values are the things you find most important in a relationship. When you familiarize yourself with these, you'll be able to communicate them to your partner and will know what to look for in a relationship.

# CHAPTER 2

# Know Your Worth and Others Will Too

As a teen, there can be a *ton* of pressure to look and act a certain way. The pressures of social media make it even harder. You might feel confused and unsure about how you feel and who you think you "should" be.

Figuring out who you are and learning to feel good about yourself can be difficult, but it's *so* worth it when you get there. We're here to help you value yourself, respect yourself, and love yourself—because you deserve it! In this chapter, you will learn to identify what you're good at, pay attention to how to talk to yourself (which is something that shapes our self-esteem), and branch out with new activities, so that you can learn to value what you *do* in addition to who you think you *are*. Regardless of whether you already feel confident, or you feel like you don't measure up to others, you'll learn to build yourself up and recognize all the things that make you amazing!

Self-esteem means knowing your worth and having confidence in yourself and your abilities. Building self-esteem is an ongoing process and self-esteem is something that ebbs and flows throughout our lives. During times when you have high self-esteem, you feel really good about yourself, inside and out. During times when you have low self-esteem, you might feel bad about yourself, and lack confidence. You might compare yourself to others and feel that you aren't good enough.

For example, if you have high self-esteem and you failed your chemistry test, you might just think, "Wow, I didn't do as well as I hoped, but I'll study harder and do better next time," whereas if you have low self-esteem you might think, "I'm so stupid. I knew I could never pass that test. I'm going to fail this class for sure." As you develop your self-esteem, you'll feel like you can take on challenges, try new things, make friends, and respect yourself. Building your self-esteem happens little by little, so take your time and be patient. Soon enough you'll be able to recognize so many of your strengths!

In this chapter, you'll explore, identify, and celebrate your strengths. You will gain valuable skills to enhance your self-esteem such as practicing positive self-talk and trying new activities that might be out of your comfort zone. As you continue on this process, it's important to be aware of things that could be getting in your way. Let's look at some ways in which you may be devaluing yourself.

# Do You Compare Yourself to Others?

Sometimes it can be hard not to compare yourself to other people, especially if those people are your friends and you like and admire them. It's totally okay to admire other people and to recognize the things that make them special, but when you focus on the things that other people have that you don't, it can make you feel worse about yourself, bringing down your self-esteem.

Let's look at Liliana's experience with comparing herself to others.

Liliana is on the varsity swim team with a few of her friends. She doesn't know why, but she can't stop comparing herself to them, even though it makes her feel bad about herself. She thinks that they swim faster than she does, that they're smarter than she is, and that they're prettier than she is. She feels like people always have a crush on one of her friends, but never on her.

Sometimes she feels super self-conscious in her bathing suit. She stares at herself in the mirror, trying to figure out how to be more like them. She keeps thinking that maybe if she swims faster, studies harder, or changes something about her appearance, then maybe someone will finally want to date her.

Liliana is feeling bad about herself because she feels like she doesn't measure up to her friends, in terms of how fast she can swim, how she looks, and how popular and well-liked she is. But Liliana isn't recognizing all the amazing qualities she has—and the more she compares herself to her teammates, the worse she feels.

Maybe your problem isn't comparing yourself to others, but trying to be perfect. You might think that if you were just perfect, you'd feel better about yourself. Although perfectionism might seem like it can motivate you to reach your goals, sometimes it actually makes you feel worse about yourself, if you can't meet your own expectations. While it's okay to work on yourself and have goals, it's also really important to be kind to yourself, and to recognize that you are worthy just as you are—no matter what you're "good" or "bad" at. To expect to be the best at something—or everything—isn't realistic. It could make it harder for you to do the things you enjoy, and might even pull you away from doing those things. You might start to think that if you're not the best at something, it isn't worth doing.

Our self-worth is made up of a number of qualities, including our personal attributes, our strengths, and our actions. If we focus too much on what we're "good" or "bad" at, we miss out on the whole picture. Try taking the pressure off of yourself and accepting yourself for where you are *in this moment*. Chances are, how you see yourself and how fully you live your life will improve.

Of course, self-esteem can be complicated, and it can take time and practice to feel confident. As you go through the exercises and reflections in this chapter—and across this whole book—you'll start to see how your perspective about yourself can shift. You might start to notice that you're being less critical of yourself, or not caring as much about what other people think. When you pay attention to your strengths and positive qualities, and to the things you want to do (not just "who you are," which is always changing), you'll see how being your own best friend can make all the difference.

Let's start by looking at your strengths, to learn more about how you can be the best YOU that you can be!

## *EXERCISE: LESS COMPARING, MORE STRENGTH-FINDING*

Strengths are the things that you do well and the positive qualities you have. When you spend a lot of time comparing yourself to other people, it can be hard to remember all your strengths and what makes you awesome! But when you know what your strengths are and what makes you unique, it's much easier to discover all that you can do and achieve.

Start by asking yourself the following reflection questions:

What am I good at?

What positive qualities do I have?

How have I used my positive qualities and abilities?

What have my strengths allowed me to do in my life so far?

Have any qualities helped me to get through tough times or to help others? (For example, maybe you are good at baking cookies, your friends say you are trustworthy, or you were a good listener to a friend who was having a hard time.)

Grab your journal and make a list of all of your strengths—and keep it somewhere where you can read it when you need a reminder. Anytime you feel down about yourself, or catch yourself comparing yourself to others, you can review your strengths and remind yourself of all that you have going for you.

## Being Your Own Best Friend

Sometimes it can be hard not to speak negatively to yourself, especially if you're experiencing a disappointment, failure, or unrequited romantic feelings. While many of us experience sadness and disappointment when something doesn't work out, and it's normal to feel strongly about things you really care about, how well you perform shouldn't damage your overall self-worth.

Let's look at Keiko's experience.

*Keiko has always loved theater and her favorite class is drama. Recently, she spent hours memorizing her lines for an audition for the school play. She felt like she did well at the audition and was hoping to get the lead—but she just found out that she got a small non-speaking role instead. This was a major setback for her and she started questioning everything.*

*She keeps thinking, "I can't believe I didn't get the part—I must not be as good as I thought," and "Maybe I shouldn't even be in the play if I'm not good enough to get a speaking part."*

It's very common to feel like your self-worth is defined by how other people see you or what they think of you. In fact, it's a normal part of development to care what people think about us! We all reach a point around adolescence where we realize we're part of larger groups, and then try to figure out how we'll fit in with the people around us and in the world. But when we experience a disappointment or setback, it's easy to forget that the most important thing to work on is how you see *yourself*. When you feel good about yourself, it gives you confidence and helps you to feel more secure, whatever might happen in your life or the world around you.

The goal here is to be your own best friend and reach a level of self-acceptance. Having self-acceptance means that you accept yourself as you are, with both your strengths and areas for growth. It can take time to develop self-acceptance—in fact, it's something you'll keep working on your whole life; we all do, as we deal with whatever life brings us. But it can be very freeing to experience! It means that you have the freedom to be yourself without having to second-guess anything you're doing, question what others think of you, or wonder if you're measuring up to standards set by someone else.

Sometimes, when you experience a disappointment, you might start to think negatively about yourself or say critical things to yourself like Keiko did. This is important to pay attention to and work on, so that you don't do any damage to your self-esteem.

Let's take a look at the next exercise, which will help you to pay attention to how you talk to yourself, and to reframe your thoughts.

## EXERCISE: PRACTICING POSITIVE SELF-TALK

Self-talk is the way that you talk to yourself in your head. We all do it! Sometimes the things we say to ourselves are positive, but often they can be negative. You can turn a negative voice into a positive voice with these three steps:

The first step is to start paying attention to the way that you talk to yourself. Are you saying nice things? If so, keep it up!

If not, the second step is to challenge those thoughts. By challenging the unhelpful thoughts that you're having, you are taking steps to create more helpful thoughts. Ask yourself if there's any real evidence for whatever it is that you're telling yourself. Are you looking at your situation accurately? Or are you letting feelings or assumptions that maybe aren't accurate distort how you see your situation or yourself?

Try asking, "Is that how I would talk to a friend?" to see if what you're saying to yourself is actually helpful or kind. (While it's a common belief that we can punish ourselves into doing or being better, in the long run—as you've probably noticed if you've ever given anyone advice or support—you do better and feel better when you're kind to yourself, even at times when you're trying to change or improve).

If you notice that you're not talking to yourself kindly, the third step is to imagine how you can talk to yourself like your own best friend.

Take a look at the examples on the following page for some ways to change your self-talk.

| Negative Self-Talk | Challenging the Beliefs | Positive Self-Talk |
| --- | --- | --- |
| "I'm so ugly. No one will ever like me." | Would I call one of my friends ugly? Is it true that no one will ever like me? | "I think my eyes are pretty. I haven't dated anyone yet, but that doesn't mean no one will ever like me." |
| "I knew I was going to fail that test. I'm so stupid." | Wow, I'm being harsh on myself! Would I tell that to a friend if she failed? | "Just because I failed, that doesn't mean that I'm not intelligent. I'll study harder for the next test." |
| "I'll never run as fast as the other girls on the varsity team." | Is this true? What evidence do I have that I'll never be able to run as fast as them? | "Coach chose me to be on varsity for a reason, and I know that if I keep training, I'll get even faster." |
| "I hate my arms. They look so ugly in tank tops." | Is it fair to talk to myself this way? Would I ever talk like that to my best friend? | "It doesn't matter what my arms look like. They do so much for me! They let me walk my dog and play my guitar." |

Once you've gained an awareness of how you talk to yourself and you've started to challenge those thoughts, you can start to change the way that you speak to yourself. Pretty soon it will become second nature.

So, what can Keiko do? Keiko feels insecure about herself and "not good enough." She can build up her confidence and self-esteem by remembering her strengths and paying attention to the way that she talks to herself. This will help her to remember and acknowledge her positive qualities, so that she isn't so focused on her recent setback.

But what about the play? Once Keiko builds up her self-esteem, she may start to feel like it's not as important what role she has or what other people think of her. Even though she may still feel disappointed, she'll be able to recognize her strengths despite her disappointment. She can learn that it's possible to make the best out of a disappointment: to still have fun and learn from the process.

Experiencing disappointments, failures, and setbacks is a normal part of growing up and it happens to everyone! Remember that you are enough, just as you are. You can't control what happens and, whatever happens, it's not a reflection of your self-worth.

We all have strengths and positive qualities that make us unique. We also are all human, and we have flaws too. While it's okay to work on self-improvement (gaining new skills, trying new things, exploring your identity), other people's opinions do not define you. We shouldn't try to change ourselves—especially not in a way that doesn't align with our values. No one is perfect, and we shouldn't try to be!

# Do You Stop Yourself from Trying New Things?

It's normal to be nervous about meeting new people, trying new things, or going new places, especially if you struggle with your self-esteem and how you see yourself. You might wonder what people will think of you, if you'll be as good at the thing you want to try as the people around you, or if you'll like or fit in at the place you want to visit. Ultimately, though, the only way to get better at something, or to find out if you like something, is to try it. And if you want to live a full life that's really rewarding, you'll need to take some risks and try some things that might not feel comfortable at first.

While it might be easier and more comfortable to stay home, having healthy self-esteem will keep you from letting nervousness stop you from going after what you want. You can also bring a healthy sense of self-awareness to the things you want to do. If you're not ready yet, that's okay too. Take your time, and branch out when you feel ready!

It's very common to want to avoid things that are new and unfamiliar, especially if you think you don't quite have what it takes. Maybe there's a club you want to join but you don't know anyone in it. Maybe you really like Spanish class but you never participate because you worry people will laugh at how you pronounce things. Maybe you want to ask someone out but you're afraid they'll say no.

Again, while avoiding these things might seem like the easier option, it's not always one that feels good—because in the long run, it can keep you from doing things that would really be meaningful to you, and might make you feel happy or fulfilled. Also, one of the best ways to build your self-esteem is to try new things, improve your skills, and learn through experience. You might just realize that often, you can do more than you think you can!

When we experience life to the fullest, it feels really good. Will you be great at every single thing you try? Of course not! But you won't know unless you do at least try. And remember when we talked about perfectionism? You don't have to be perfect at something in order to enjoy it.

Of course, building your skills and confidence will take time and practice. The process is a challenge—but it's a healthy one. When you build your skills, overcome challenges, and connect with others in the process, it's a major self-esteem boost.

So, what should you do the next time you're scared to do something because you don't feel good enough at it? Check in with yourself first. Are you remembering your strengths? Are you practicing positive self-talk? Are you accepting yourself for where you're at right now—or are you trying to be perfect? If you find that you're picturing all the things that can go wrong, you might try instead picturing all the things that could go well—and how it could benefit your life either way. Many challenging situations we find ourselves in teach us things, even if they don't go the way we might hope.

Although it's common to feel nervous about trying new things, especially if you're struggling with self-esteem, the benefits of trying are often *huge*. Sometimes the things that are the hardest to do are the most rewarding!

Let's take a look at the next exercise, which will help you think of ways you can branch out and improve your self-esteem.

## EXERCISE: BRANCH OUT AND TRY NEW THINGS

Since you've already begun identifying your strengths and practicing positive self-talk, it's time to start branching out and trying new things. When you meet new people, develop new skills, and engage fully with life, it will help you to feel good about yourself. So, let's put aside the phone, turn off Netflix, and start thinking of some branches you can climb out on!

Start by asking yourself the following questions:

What are some things I'm already doing that make me feel good about myself?

Who are people that I hang out with that make me feel good about myself?

What are some things/places/activities/clubs/sports/interests I'd like to try?

Next, grab a piece of paper and start drawing a big tree with lots of branches (it doesn't have to look perfect!). On the lower branches of the tree, write the names of people, places, and activities that make you feel good about yourself. Each branch represents one thing—these are things that you are already connected to. On the higher branches of the tree, write down some things you'd like to try in the future that you haven't tried yet.

Now take a look at the tree and see how you feel. This tree represents the way you've grown so far and the way you'll grow in the future. And you know what's cool about trees? They keep growing new branches, and they're always there for you to explore!

## Let's Recap: Knowing Your Worth

Building your self-esteem and acknowledging your self-worth is an ongoing process. Remember this recap as you continue on this journey:

**Self-Esteem:** Having high self-esteem means feeling good about yourself and knowing that you are worthy. You can improve your self-esteem by identifying your strengths, practicing positive self-talk, and spending time with people who care about you. Engage in activities that make you feel good about yourself!

**Perfectionism:** Perfectionism is when you try really hard to be great at something and put a lot of pressure on yourself in the process. Although it might seem like a good thing, sometimes it can make you feel worse, when you can't meet your own expectations. Practice being kind to yourself and recognizing that you are worthy even if you aren't the best at something.

**Self-Acceptance:** When you love and accept yourself, you'll realize that the opinions of others don't define you. You are enough, right here, right now. And true friends, family, and romantic partners will appreciate you for *you*—both your strengths and your flaws.

# CHAPTER 3

# Sexual "I"dentity Celebrates Who You Are

Your identity—or "I"dentity—has so many aspects: your interests, cultural background, ethnicity, religious or spiritual beliefs, family, and passions (just to name a few). One of the most significant parts of your identity is your sexual identity.

Your sexual identity includes your sexual orientation—who you are attracted to sexually or want to share sexual experiences with. Another aspect of your identity is your gender identity—which gender you identify as, or if you identify as any one gender at all.

In this chapter, we'll discuss the spectrum of sexual identity and offer exercises to encourage self-exploration and celebration of your own identity. We'll also discuss some of the challenges you may face during this self-exploration, and help you develop skills to cope with potential roadblocks.

## Understanding Identity

Your sexual orientation is an important aspect of your identity, because it usually influences who you date or have relationships with; who you love and are intimate with. You could be attracted to the opposite gender, or to the same gender, or both; or maybe you don't have a preference either way. Some people truly fall in love with or are attracted to the *person* and their gender is insignificant. You also might not experience sexual attraction at all or have any interest in being physically intimate with another person.

For some, sexuality is unchanging—you are sure of who you like and are sexually attracted to. For others, one's sexuality is fluid; it changes. What is important to remember is that your sexual identity or orientation is unique to you. Who you love and/or are attracted to is part of who you are. Whether you are straight, gay, lesbian, bisexual, queer, pansexual, asexual, or choose not to define yourself at all, you are perfect as you are, and you deserve to be you in every way!

Take a second to read through some definitions for terms of identities below. As you read, see which ones you do and don't identify with, and which ones feel like they best describe you. The following quoted material comes from the Gay and Lesbian Alliance Against Defamation (GLAAD) website.

**Gay:** A term used by some individuals "whose enduring physical, romantic, and/or emotional attractions are to people of the same sex."

**Lesbian:** A term sometimes preferred by women "whose enduring physical, romantic, and/or emotional attraction is to other women."

**Bisexual:** A term sometimes used by an individual "who has the capacity to form enduring physical, romantic, and/or emotional attractions to those of the same gender or to those of another gender." You don't need to have specific romantic or sexual experiences to be bisexual. You might also experience bisexual attraction in differing ways and degrees over the course of your life.

**Queer:** A term used by some "whose sexual orientation is not exclusively heterosexual (e.g. queer person, queer woman)."

**Asexual:** A term used to describe the identity of "people who do not experience sexual attraction."

**Heterosexual:** A term used to describe individuals "whose enduring physical, romantic, and/or emotional attraction is to people of the opposite sex. Also *straight*."

Your identity also includes the gender that you identify as ("gender identity") and how you express it. At birth, your gender is determined based on the sex organs that you are born with. This is the gender that is assigned to you at birth.

Then there is the gender that *you* identify as—your actual, personal gender identity. Sometimes the gender that has been assigned to you aligns with your personal gender identity and sometimes it does not. For example, you can be assigned "female" at birth and also identify as "female" or "woman." If your gender does not align, you could be assigned "male" at birth but identify as "female" or "woman." It is also possible that neither gender ("female"/"woman" or "male"/"man") fits or reflects who you are, and you might identify as "non-binary" or "gender-nonconforming."

Part of your gender identity includes your personal pronouns—the words that are used to refer to another individual (i.e. "she," "he," "they"). Identifying and claiming personal pronouns can be an important aspect of your identity, because these reflect how you identify (which may be different than the gender you were assigned at birth). For example, if you were assigned female at birth and identify as female, you are probably comfortable and identify with female pronouns, "she/her." If you were assigned female at birth but identify as male, your personal pronouns could be "he/him." Or, if you were assigned female at birth but identify as non-binary or gender-nonconforming, you may identify with the gender-neutral pronouns "they/them." It's also possible that none of these pronouns accurately reflect your gender identity or how you identify. If this is the case, there are other pronouns you might use (i.e. "ze"). Other individuals use only their name as their personal pronoun.

In addition to your gender identity, how you express your gender is also personal and can be unique to you. Gender expression is how you present yourself outwardly to others. This can include how you dress, your behavior, and the things you're interested in. So, know that while you may identify as "female"/"woman," you can express yourself in ways that are feminine, masculine, or androgynous (neither specifically masculine or feminine).

And how you express and present your gender can stay the same or change. For instance, in time, you might come to find that the labels "female" and "woman" don't actually define you the way you once thought they did. Or you might find your gender expression changes—becomes more masculine, more feminine, more androgynous, or something else.

**Bottom line:** your identity is your own and you have the right to be who you are and express yourself in a way that is true and authentic! Check out the exercise below, which can help you explore your sexual identity.

## EXERCISE: EXPLORE YOUR SEXUAL IDENTITY

Everyone has their own path when it comes to understanding and exploring their identity. One person might be very clear about who they are and how they identify, while another might be unsure and need more time and experience to explore and determine their sexual identity. It's also true that sexual identity isn't necessarily something fixed; yours might evolve in any number of ways over the course of your life.

There is no right or wrong way to go about exploring these aspects of your identity, but following are some questions that you can ask yourself and reflect on. You can respond to these questions in your journal or just think about them on your own.

1. Who are you typically attracted to? What is your "type"?
2. Are you comfortable with your sexuality? Why or why not?
3. Are there parts of your identity that you feel uncomfortable sharing? Are there parts of your sexuality that you feel like you have to hide? Why?
4. Are you unsure about any aspects of your sexual orientation or gender expression? How might you start to explore this? Who could you talk to?
5. Are there parts of your sexuality that you are confident in? Why or why not? What might you need to feel more confident?

Again, if there are questions you don't yet know the answers to, or answers you aren't quite sure of, this isn't a problem. These are complex issues, but when you make time to self-reflect and think about parts of you, it can create more self-awareness, helping you to navigate situations and relationships with more confidence and ease.

## Opening up about Your Sexual Identity

Being open and sharing aspects of your sexual identity with others can be difficult, specifically around sensitive topics such as one's relationship history and sexual orientation, or one's beliefs and values related to sex. For some people, there can be a lot of worry about whether or not their partner, friends, and family will accept them, and how they will be treated. Some people in the LGBTQIA+ community might even worry about getting kicked out of their home or disowned by their family, friends, or community if they open up about their sexuality.

Ultimately, how and when you share aspects of your sexual identity with others is solely up to you. This is your identity and only yours to share. Let's take a look at Avery's experience.

*Avery finally told her friend Lexi that she liked her and would like to be in a relationship. It was really hard to do because, until recently, nobody at their school knew Avery was gay. Lexi, meanwhile, is openly gay. She has a family that is super accepting, and is active in her Gender and Sexuality Alliance (GSA) club.*

*And now Avery and Lexi are going out! Generally, the relationship is going pretty well, but Avery is envious of how open Lexi is. Even though Avery's friends now know she's gay, she isn't sure if she's ready to come out to anyone else yet. She's pretty sure her family knows, but when she thinks about coming out to them she gets really nervous.*

Opening up to others about your gender identity and sexual orientation should always happen on your own terms. It should not be something you feel forced to do, or do out of obligation—even for your partner. Coming out as LGBTQIA+ is also usually not just a single conversation—for a lot of people it's an ongoing experience and process. People come out at all ages and stages of their life and it can look different for everyone. Some people have to consider their safety and the amount of support they have before safely coming out.

Going back to the situation with Avery, while Avery believes her parents *might* know that she is gay, she isn't necessarily ready to come out, and that is OKAY. She needs to do what feels best and most safe for her.

Avery could try and seek support from others like her at school or online. She could also seek support from a therapist or trusted adult, someone who she could process this with in a safe space. (And just a heads up, anything that you share in therapy—as long as you are not in danger in some way that your therapist will have a duty to report—is completely confidential, even if you are a minor.)

If you are considering opening up about your sexual identity, you get to decide when, where, and with whom. You may share this part of you with a close friend but decide that you are not ready to open up to your family. It's completely up to you! Remember that you are not alone, and there are so many wonderful resources and people you can go to for support (please see the resources at the back of this book for more info). It's okay to seek help and it can feel empowering to do so.

## When Others Don't Understand Your Gender Identity

Some families continue to value and maintain traditional gender roles and gender expression. A lot of our society still sees gender as strictly binary, meaning it's one or the other. If you are "male," you behave and dress in a way that is traditionally "masculine." And if you are "female," you behave and dress in a way that is more "feminine." It can be difficult for some communities and people to see gender and gender expression as something fluid and/or unique to each individual, which can make it really difficult for some to embrace their true self and express themselves in a way that feels real.

Let's take a look at Laura's experience.

*Laura recently asked their family to use gender-neutral pronouns, "they/them," when they reference Laura, because it more accurately reflects their gender identity. Laura's mom has been resistant to this, and has been also giving them a hard time for only wearing jeans and T-shirts. Laura's mom tries to buy Laura more "girly" clothes like dresses and revealing shirts, and she always talks about how much more beautiful Laura would be if they dressed differently. While Laura recognizes that their mom is probably uncomfortable with their gender expression because it's not what she's used to or what she might've wanted for her child, it doesn't make it any easier. They want to be accepted by their mom for who they are.*

Laura identifies as non-binary and uses "they/them" pronouns. They like to wear jeans and T-shirts—this is their style, how they like to express their gender, and what they feel most confident in. Their mom, however, doesn't seem to like or understand their lack of femininity and believes that Laura should dress and present in a certain way—a more "feminine" way. Laura's mom seems to be questioning her child's right and ability to determine their own gender identity and self-presentation, as well as having her own opposing beliefs about gender identity. While Laura's mom is most likely not intentionally trying to hurt Laura's feelings or make them feel bad,

Laura is having a hard time and doesn't feel truly accepted or understood.

So, what can Laura do? Laura can try to set boundaries with their mom and respectfully explain that how they dress is up to them and what they are most comfortable in. They can also try to explain how the pressure to dress a certain way makes them feel bad about themselves and rejected for who they are. These conversations can be difficult to initiate and require bravery, but can sometimes help to provide more understanding.

Laura could also seek support through another family member, therapist, or friend. Laura doesn't need to change or be something that they are not. How they dress and express themselves is totally up to them.

What if you don't feel accepted by a family member or someone you love? Or what if a loved one questions something that is important or meaningful to you and who you are? If possible, you can try to talk to this person and express how you are feeling, or try to set boundaries. However, we recognize that it might not always feel safe or comfortable to have these types of conversations. If that's the case, try to reach out to a friend or different family member for some emotional support.

It can feel incredibly lonely sometimes when you are misunderstood, but remember, you are enough exactly as you are, and you're not alone.

Give yourself lots of love and make sure that you stay true to who you are!

## EXERCISE: EXPRESSING YOURSELF USING "I" STATEMENTS

Expressing how you are feeling and what you need from a family member or loved one can feel uncomfortable, especially around sensitive topics and conversations like your sexuality or gender identity. "I" statements can be a helpful tool to communicate your thoughts and feelings in a way that is firm and direct but not accusatory. (Sentences that start with "You" tend to feel accusatory and can make people get defensive.) For example, instead of saying "You never listen to me," you could say "I don't feel heard."

"I" statements are effective because they allow you to express how another person's actions or behaviors have impacted or affected you, without assuming that the other person had bad intentions. For example, in the situation between Laura and their mom, Laura could use "I" statements to communicate how their mom's actions are hurting their feelings.

Here are some examples of "I" statements:

> I don't feel cared about when my pronouns aren't used correctly or when I'm misgendered.

I don't feel safe when I'm getting yelled at.

I feel really insecure about myself when people make jokes about me.

Use the following sentence structure to make your own "I" statements:

I feel _____, when _____.
When _____, I feel _____.

"I" statements can feel awkward to use at first, but with time and practice they will come naturally. And as you practice this skill more and more, pay attention to how the other person responds. You'll probably notice that they are less defensive and more open to feedback.

Now let's discuss how to navigate situations in which you feel judged by others for your sexual identity.

# When You Are Judged for Your Sexuality

Our society still hasn't quite figured out how to navigate and respond to strong, empowered women who know who they are. It might not always be easy to claim your sexuality (your sexual feelings and expressions) or share it with others. There are cultural and societal beliefs and prejudices that may make it hard to accept, embrace, or express your authentic self. You may have fear of rejection from your culture, family, community, or school.

At the end of the day, there are a few truths to keep in mind. One, it is a process to get to know who you are. Know that it can take time to feel fully empowered in your sexuality, and fully able to embrace it. Give yourself the time you need to get to know what you feel, what you want, and who you really are.

Two, know that who you are, whoever that happens to be, is enough. It's hard not to feel like your worth comes down to how other people see you—especially the people you love and care about. And if they're ever the ones judging you, it can be incredibly painful and destabilizing. But even in these painful circumstances, you can know your truth and embrace it, as best you can.

And three, you can always seek out support from the friends and loved ones who accept you for who you are. Don't be afraid to use local resources like counseling and therapy—perhaps through community centers and support groups in your area—or to find support online if it's hard to find services where you are. (See the Resources list at the back of this book for more information about these options, if you need them.)

Let's look at what happened to Phoenix when she opened up to her boyfriend, Marco, about her sexuality.

*Phoenix has been with her boyfriend Marco for four months. Things had been going well, so recently Phoenix opened up about who she is and told him about her past partners before him. Marco got upset and started to question their relationship and Phoenix's commitment to him. He now sometimes acts suspicious about where she's been in a way he wasn't before, and he worries she might be looking at other guys. Phoenix thinks he's probably just insecure because this is his first relationship, while she has had more experience.*

Phoenix was just trying to be open and honest about who she is, and now she's feeling judged for her relationship history. We don't know what Marco is thinking or feeling, but it seems like he may be feeling insecure because he has less experience. Phoenix is frustrated by his response and she feels like he doesn't accept her for who she is.

Let's be clear: in this situation, Phoenix did *everything* right. She was open and vulnerable—which can be a very difficult thing to do, especially if you don't know how another person will respond or react, and *especially* if the person you're talking to is someone you like, or even love.

She's not ashamed of who she is and the choices she's made. She's learning and growing and these experiences are part of her journey. And while Marco may be in his feelings about what she's told him, she should understand that

that's his own stuff and not her responsibility. She can try to initiate an honest conversation with Marco about his insecurities, to see if they can work to resolve them. And maybe he'll come around as a result—or maybe he won't. If Marco continues to struggle with Phoenix's relationship history and holds that against her, then she can consider whether this relationship is best for her.

So, what can you do if someone questions or challenges your ability to make decisions for yourself about your sexuality? It's often wise to have honest conversations with your partners about both of your pasts—especially if you plan to be sexually active. But don't feel obligated to do this, especially if your partner is pressuring you or judging you aggressively for what you disclose to them. Sharing each other's histories, relationship or otherwise, is part of getting to know one another in any committed relationship. But it has to be done with kindness and mutual respect. You deserve that.

## Let's Recap: Identity

Exploring and understanding your sexual identity is a process and can take time. Expressing and sharing this part of yourself with others should be done on your terms and when it feels safe. There may be times when you feel judged or rejected for who you are—and while this can be difficult, what is most important is that you accept and show up for yourself unconditionally.

**Sexuality/Sexual Orientation:** This is how we see ourselves as sexual beings, as well as who we are attracted to sexually or want to share sexual experiences with. Your sexuality can be fluid and it can change over time. So, remember that there is no "wrong" or "right" way when it comes to your sexuality, and that you are allowed to be exactly who you are.

**Gender Identity:** Your gender identity is determined by YOU. You can identify as female, male, or non-binary, or you may not consider gender as part of your identity at all. Like sexual orientation, gender identity can be fluid. You get to claim your pronouns and how you express your gender identity.

**You Are Enough:** Who you are is enough. Your identity is yours to determine. If there's someone in your life who is expressing doubt or judgment about your identity, it may be very hard to deal with—but it should never be a reason for you to doubt or judge yourself for your identity, or to downplay it, or try to change it. Get the support you need to be the person you are, without shame or apology.

# CHAPTER 4

# Your Own Body Love Comes First

Do you feel good about yourself and the way that you look? Maybe there are some parts of you that you like a lot, and other parts that you like a little less, or even not at all. However you feel about your body, it's okay. Our bodies go through a lot of physical changes, and it can feel hard to appreciate those changes sometimes. When you add in all of the pressures of society and social media, it can feel even harder.

What would it feel like to look in the mirror and really love what you see, without critique, commentary, or criticism? Learning to love your body and to develop a healthy body image is an important part of getting older. It's important to think about our body image—the ways we think and feel about our bodies—and whether it's healthy.

When you have a healthy body image, you feel confident about the way your body looks, you wear clothes that make you feel good, and you appreciate everything your body can do for you. When you have an unhealthy body image, you may feel self-conscious, you may criticize yourself, and you may even try unhealthy things to change your appearance (more on this later). You might compare yourself to others, in person and on social media, and feel bad about yourself.

As you develop a healthy body image, you'll be able to feel more comfortable and confident. You only get one body, so let's start appreciating it! Let's look at some ways you might be struggling with body image, and how to help. In this chapter, we'll explore what to do when your body's changing and you're not sure how to feel about it, when you see specific parts of your body you dislike, and when you feel self-conscious about your weight, in particular—a common experience among teen girls especially. And you'll learn techniques to soothe yourself in times of pain, build your body confidence, and love your body and all that it can do for you.

## Do You Struggle to Accept Your Body's Changes?

As you get older, your body goes through many changes. Let's take a look at Asha's experience with struggling to accept her body as it changes.

> Asha really hates the way her body has been changing. When she was in elementary school she felt just like everyone else, but now she feels so different. She started wearing a bra way before her friends, she feels like her jeans never fit her right, and it seems like guys

*are always staring at her. Her mom tells her that in their family, the women believe that it's beautiful to be curvy, but when Asha goes on social media and looks at influencers' posts, she notices that none of them look like her—and they get so many likes on their posts. She wears baggy sweatshirts all the time to cover up (even when it's hot) because she doesn't like the way people look at her.*

Throughout adolescence (and your whole life!), your body continues to change and grow. Some of us will really love the ways our body is changing. For others, it can be uncomfortable. Either way, it can take a while to accept yourself and appreciate all the changes your body is going through. It's very common to go through times when you feel great about yourself, and then other times when you feel less confident. It's also important to recognize that you are so much more than a number on a scale or a cup size. Your body is amazing and it can do SO many things for you! And there's more to who "you" are than just your body.

You might also notice that as you get older, you're getting more attention from people who are attracted to you. This can be fun and exciting, and it can also be awkward and uncomfortable if you don't want that attention. Remember that getting and expressing feelings of attraction are a normal part of growing up. It can also take some getting used to. And, while it's normal for people to feel attraction, it's not okay to objectify someone for their looks or to make sexualized comments about someone's appearance. If anyone ever makes you feel uncomfortable or unsafe by making rude comments, bullying you, harassing you, or physically harming you, make sure you talk to an adult about what's going on.

Social media can also really affect a person's self-esteem and body image. With a combination of angles, filters, makeup contouring, and editing, a person's post can look completely different from how they look in real life! That person who you think looks perfect online might have taken a couple hundred selfies and applied lots of different filters before they chose the version they liked.

Some people also feel bad if they don't have many followers or get many "likes" on their posts. This makes it so important to remember that what you see on social media or in movies and on TV isn't reality. If you find that what you see online or in movies/TV is making you feel insecure, try going back to your list of strengths from Chapter 2, to remind yourself of your positive qualities.

Back to Asha's story. Rather than spending her time comparing herself to girls who don't look like her, Asha can learn more about body positivity. Body positivity is a movement that celebrates bodies of all shapes, colors, and sizes. Instead of comparing herself to influencers who look nothing like her, she could follow some body-positive accounts on social media, so that she feels like she can relate more to what she sees online. She can also choose to log off sometimes—to limit the amount of time she spends online.

Asha's mom told her that in their family, curves are really appreciated and celebrated. There are many views on women's beauty and women's expressions of beauty. Asha might like to spend more time with the women in her family, to learn more about celebrating the aspects of her appearance that make her unique.

Unfortunately, Asha's experience of unwanted attention isn't uncommon. Women and girls continue to be objectified and sometimes face situations including staring, unwanted compliments, or catcalling. What can Asha do about this?

First of all, it's important that she feels safe and comfortable, and like she has the right to wear whatever clothes she feels good in. So, when it comes time to pick out an outfit for the day, she can ask herself, "Does this outfit make me feel comfortable and good about myself?"

If she gets comments or looks that make her uneasy, she can choose to confront the person (if she's comfortable with that and it feels safe to). Or she can remind herself that what other people do is *their* responsibility, not hers.

As Asha becomes more confident in herself and her appearance, her level of comfort and her style might change. She might start to feel like she doesn't really care what other people think! She might even stop noticing whether people look at her because she is busy focusing on whatever she is doing. And of course, if anyone makes her feel unsafe, she should tell an adult.

How can you cope when someone makes you feel uncomfortable about your body? Here are some ideas of things you can do when others make you feel uncomfortable:

Remind yourself that you can't control what other people say or do, and that their actions are not a reflection of you or your worth.

Talk to a friend about how unwanted attention makes you feel—maybe they can relate.

Journal about your feelings and your experiences as a young woman in our society.

Confront the person about how their comments affect you (if you feel safe to do so).

Tell an adult if someone makes you feel unsafe.

While it's common during the teenage years to struggle with body image and to feel some discomfort or insecurity with the way your body changes, developing a healthy body image is a process and can take time. It's important not to rush it and not to put too much pressure on yourself. The way we feel about our bodies can also be affected by the attention that we receive from others. Through the exercises in this chapter, you'll start to recognize the amazingness of your body, no matter what shape or size or color it comes in!

## EXERCISE: BODY IMAGE

So how can you improve your body image? Try shifting your focus to the things you appreciate about your body, rather than how it compares to others'. Grab a piece of paper and answer the following reflection questions:

What are the things that I like about myself and about my body?

Example: I share the same eyes as my mom, I am strong, I like that I am biracial and have qualities from both of my cultures.

What are all the things that my body can do for me?

Example: My legs help me run fast, I am grateful for my heart and lungs, which allow me to breathe each day.

How do I treat my body? What nice things do I do for my body to take care of myself?

Example: I like to put on scented lotion after a shower, I like to paint my nails and put on a face mask.

# Feeling Uncomfortable in Your Own Skin

Sometimes when you look in the mirror, it can be hard not to notice all the little things about your body that don't look the way you think they should—even if you feel confident about yourself. Since the world is full of photoshopping, makeup contouring, filters, angles, and lighting, it can be hard to remember that imperfections are actually very common and we all have them! If you find you're struggling to accept how specific aspects of your body look, we're here to help. Let's look at Emma's experience.

*Emma has been getting a lot of acne on her face and back. She's tried a million cleansers and creams, but nothing works. Her mom took her to the dermatologist and that kind of helped, but the acne is still there and she feels like she has to wear a lot of makeup every day just to leave the house. The last time she had a really bad breakout, she didn't even want to see her friends, especially because this guy she was talking to was going to be there, but her mom made her go anyway. She ended up crying in the bathroom while she was getting ready and when she looked in the mirror she thought, "This is so disgusting. I hate my skin."*

Emma is dealing with acne, an issue that affects many teens. It's common to care about what you look like and how people see you. But that doesn't mean that it has to take a negative toll on your mental health. There are a lot of ways that you can feel good about your body and improve your self-image, even if you are dealing with parts of your body that you don't like.

When it comes to your appearance, you might be putting a lot of pressure on yourself to look a certain way. That pressure can be really overwhelming and exhausting, especially if you aren't able to meet your own expectations for how you want to look. Sometimes the pressure can even make you feel depressed, like you can't enjoy your life.

Having a healthy body image means that you accept yourself as you are, with both the qualities of your appearance that you like, and the ones you don't. It can take time to get there, and we'll help you along the way. While there's absolutely nothing wrong with wanting to enhance your appearance (wearing makeup, experimenting with different outfits, changing your hairstyle, and adding filters to pics), it's important to do these things because they make you feel *good*, not because you're feeling bad. For example, there's a difference between wearing makeup because it makes you feel confident vs. wearing it because you think you'll get more attention on your social media post. See the difference?

Emma is feeling terrible about her skin. She has already taken some good steps by going to the doctor and taking care of her health. But she's still struggling, which is affecting her emotions and making her want to isolate. After Emma reminds herself of all the good things her body can do for her, she can practice some self-soothing techniques, to focus her attention elsewhere and help her to feel comfortable in her own skin. She can also talk to a trusted adult for emotional support, especially in the moments when it's hard to self-soothe, so that her thoughts about her skin don't keep her from enjoying her life.

If you're ever in a situation where your body image is affecting your emotions, you can do the same thing. Let's take a look at the next exercise, which will help you learn how to soothe yourself when you get stuck in negative thoughts about your body, so you can learn to feel good in your own body.

## EXERCISE: SELF-SOOTHING

Self-soothing has to do with being kind and nurturing to yourself. It's a way to feel calm, relaxed, and safe in your body. Self-soothing exercises can relate to the senses and include sight, taste, smell, hearing, and touch. For this exercise, we'll focus on the self-soothing that relates to touch, since that can help your body to physically and mentally feel better.

Here are some examples of self-soothing techniques to try that will feel good for your body and heart. As you practice these exercises, pay attention to how they feel, and you may even want to thank your body for the good feelings.

Wrap yourself up in your coziest, fluffiest blanket.

Take a warm bubble bath.

Gently rub some nice-smelling moisturizer on your hands and breathe in the scent.

Lie down with your hands on your heart and take slow, deep breaths.

Cuddle with your pet or favorite stuffed animal.

Give yourself a hug.

Add your own to the list! There are lots more ways for you to feel comfortable and good in your body. Practice what works for you.

Self-soothing can help you dial down negative thoughts and feelings about your body and shift your perspective. Will it change your appearance? Nope. But when you feel good and comfortable in your body, you won't be so focused on changing it.

You can also self-soothe using affirmations. When we find we're stuck in negative thoughts about how our bodies *look*, it can be useful to move our focus to what our bodies *do* for us—to the many advantages of having a body, which it can be so easy to lose sight of. Using what you learned from the body image exercise earlier in the chapter, practice statements you can say to yourself when you want to turn on the self-love. For example, when Emma's thoughts about her skin get particularly persistent, she could shift her focus to how her body helps her when she's doing something she enjoys: I love that my body can make great serves in volleyball. She knows that when she's on the court, she's not thinking about her skin at all; she's just enjoying the feeling of playing the game.

## Do You Worry About Your Weight?

Over the course of thousands of years, beauty standards for women have changed across generations and cultures. Even within the past few decades, the portrayal of women's beauty standards has changed dramatically in the media. For teen girls (and adults!), this can be very confusing and can cause a lot of pressure.

When it comes to women's bodies, it seems like society can't make up its mind. The messaging changes constantly. Be very thin. No, wait, be fit and strong. No, actually, be curvy with large boobs and butts. But wait—not too curvy! Not too short, not too tall. Have a flat stomach, but with meat on your bones.

Sound familiar? It's too much! You might wonder how to deal with all this pressure to look a certain way. Let's take a look at Jada's experience.

*Jada grew up with a mom who was always dieting. For as long as she can remember, her mom was always trying different diets and complaining about her weight. When Jada was little, she didn't really worry about her body, but now that she's getting older, she's starting to have thoughts about her body that sound like what she's grown up hearing from her mom. It doesn't help that her mom has been making comments about Jada's weight too.*

*Jada tries to be healthy by exercising and eating healthy foods, but her friend Gen just started a diet and Jada is wondering if she should too. She feels like maybe guys would give her more attention if she lost weight.*

It's important to actively resist the pressure to conform to someone else's ideal. Your body is *yours*, no one else's. No one can tell you how it should look—not your mom, family, friends, celebrities, influencers, or anyone else!

Growing up hearing certain messages can affect how you feel about your body as it's changing. It can be easy to internalize the messages that you hear from your parents, or other adults who make comments about people's weight—for those messages to become part of the way you think about yourself and others. Jada's mom, for instance, has been dieting and complaining about her weight for as long as Jada can remember. Unfortunately, a lot of adults have internalized their own views about their bodies from their own childhood experiences and the adults *they* grew up around. They may not realize how the kinds of comments they make can affect their kids or others around them. So it's important to remember that while you may have internalized the beliefs of someone else who is struggling with their body image, you have the ability to challenge those beliefs and develop a healthier body image.

When you have a healthy body image, you also have a healthy relationship with food and exercise. You eat foods to nourish your body, you exercise because it feels good, and you feel good about the way you look. For some girls who have a negative body image, the pressure to look a certain way can cause them to engage in unhealthy eating habits or exercising behaviors. If you or someone you know is restricting their eating, trying harsh diets that weren't recommended by their doctor, exercising way too much, or anything else that seems unsafe, talk to a trusted adult for help. What you or the other person is dealing with may be too big to deal with on your own.

Jada is also feeling like she needs to change what she looks like in order to get attention from guys. Although it's normal to want people to be attracted to you, you shouldn't have to change yourself in order to get people to like you. Someone who truly likes you will like you for *all* that you are, not just what you look like.

Jada could improve her body image by practicing what we've learned, like appreciating her different body parts for what they can do for her, and self-soothing techniques to feel good in her body. She could also seek additional help if she feels that her body image is getting to the point where she is considering dieting, which could affect her overall health.

If you're in a situation like this—feeling bad about your weight, or any other part of your body—check in with yourself first. Ask yourself, "Where are these feelings coming from?" "Is this because of things I've heard family or people at school say?" "Is this because of how people look online and on TV?" When you figure out where the negative beliefs about your body are coming from, it will be easier to challenge them, and to start to appreciate the way that your body looks and everything it can do for you.

Let's take a look at the exercise below so you can try it for yourself.

## *EXERCISE: REFRAMING UNHELPFUL THOUGHTS*

Once you become aware of a negative thought that you have about yourself, you can take steps to change it by figuring out where it's coming from and reframing it. When you reframe a thought, you are changing the way that you look at a situation and gaining a more helpful perspective. Take a look at the chart below.

| Unhelpful Thought | Where Is This Coming From? | Helpful Thought Reframe |
|---|---|---|
| "I'm so fat, I hate how I look." | I overheard some girls at school calling me fat behind my back. | "Their comments don't define me. I choose to focus on what I do like about my body—like the fact that I can lift weights." |
| "I'm freakishly tall." | No one else at school is as tall as I am. | "Comparing myself to others just makes me feel worse. Being tall can be helpful. Some really great athletes are super tall too." |
| "I never smile for pictures because I hate my teeth." | Everyone I see online has perfectly straight white teeth. | "I know that a lot of pictures online are edited. I'm going to work on being grateful for all the reasons I have to smile." |

Now think of your own! Sometimes we don't even realize the negative thoughts we might have about ourselves. If you become aware of any negative thoughts, try to ask yourself where they might be coming from and practice a more helpful alternative. By reframing unhelpful thoughts, you will have more positive feelings towards your body.

Remember: despite all the conflicting messages that come your way in society, you are worth much more than what you look like. Think of some of the most amazing and inspiring women and teens in the world. People like Rosa Parks, Malala Yousafzai, Greta Thunberg, Serena Williams, Laverne Cox, and Mindy Kaling. Are they admired and celebrated because of what they look like? Nope! These teens and women are widely recognized and celebrated for their achievements in sports, politics, the creative arts, and for their contributions to society including their activism, intellectualism, athleticism, bravery, and talent.

This next exercise will help you to identify a role model, and to become aware of all the many strengths and positive qualities that women have—beyond their looks.

## EXERCISE: CHOOSING YOUR ROLE MODELS

A role model is someone we look up to, who has positive qualities that we admire. This exercise will help you to identify the role models in your life and all of the positive attributes that make them admirable.

Start by grabbing your journal and answering the following questions:

Is there a woman I know who's influenced me in a positive way? (This could be a parent, family member, teacher, coach, neighbor, or anyone else.)

Who is a woman that I've never met but look up to? (This could be a woman in politics, sports, media, or anything else.)

Who is a fictional character that I admire? (This could be a character from a book, series, or movie.)

Now that you've thought of your list of role models, think about *why* these people are inspirational to you. Describe all of the positive qualities and traits that these girls and women have that make you look up to them.

*Example:* I really look up to the rabbi at my temple. She's done a lot of good work in our community and has overcome a lot of obstacles. She is encouraging and makes time to listen to people in our community.

Once you've written your description, take a step back and see how many amazing qualities the women and girls you admire have. Many of them will have absolutely nothing to do with the size or shape of their body. Our bodies are only a small part of who we are.

Don't forget: you can let your light shine no matter what you look like.

## Let's Recap: Body Image

Loving your body and all that it can do for you is super important. It can also take time and practice. Remember this recap as you continue on this journey!

**Body image and culture:** There are a lot of physical changes during adolescence, which can sometimes make teens feel insecure. Society and mainstream media can put a lot of pressure on girls to look a certain way, and often the media doesn't reflect all ethnicities, gender presentations, shapes, and sizes. Perceptions of beauty also differ between cultures. Appreciate all the qualities that make you unique!

**Social media:** It can be really hard not to compare yourself to the images you see online. Remember that what you see online isn't reality. Also remember that no matter how many followers you have or how many likes you get on a post, what really matters are the people in the real world who care about you.

**Health and safety:** There are a lot of messages sent to girls and women about diet trends, exercise trends, cleanses, and pills. Your ultimate focus should be on your health and well-being, not changing what your body looks like. Consult with a trusted adult and doctor if you are making any changes to what you eat and how you exercise, and seek help if you or someone you know might be doing something unsafe.

# CHAPTER 5

# Choosing Your Circle of Friends

Meaningful friendships are invaluable. You know you have found "your people" when you feel seen, understood, and cared for. These people are not always easy to come by, especially at your age. But there is nothing better than having a circle of friends that accept you just as you are and support you through difficult times.

Being a girl today can be challenging at times. High school and young adulthood are already hard—and when you add technology and social media to the mix, it becomes that much harder. Girls can be so *mean* to each other. All of the comparing, exposing, and bullying can take a toll on your self-esteem and mental health. That's why it's so important to surround yourself with friends that you can trust and lean on. When you have found belonging in a circle of good friends, all the drama may seem insignificant. You'll feel more confident and self-assured and will be able to bounce back more quickly from any meanness that comes your way.

In this chapter, you will learn how to assess friendships and determine the qualities that make a good friend. We'll also discuss how friendships can change over time, and help you to develop the skills to communicate how you are feeling and speak up for yourself. We hope you'll also gain a better understanding of bullying, feel more empowered to ask for help and support, and learn ways to feel and be safer when using social media and technology.

## What Makes Someone a Good Friend?

When you were younger, your friendships might have been formed based on where you went to school, the neighborhood you lived in, or the extracurricular activities you were involved in. Many of the friends that you might have met at a younger age were probably the kids you played with and had fun being around, and maybe not so much the people you had deep or meaningful connections with.

But as you entered adolescence, you probably started noticing the different types and levels of friendships that exist. You might notice that some friendships are more superficial and based on convenience (like sharing a class together), while other friendships are deeper—ones where you can share things that are complex or hard; ones that make you feel a lot of good feelings, and possibly a lot of tough ones too. What's exciting about this age is that you also may be realizing that you get to choose who your friends are and who you surround yourself with. However, we know this isn't always easy; it can be hard to find good friends, or even to know what to look for when it comes to finding friendships that are really meaningful and satisfying.

So what makes a good friend? A good friend is reliable and trustworthy. A good friend is someone who doesn't judge you or make you feel bad about yourself. They listen to you and care about your feelings and what you have to say. And they are supportive and there for you when times are tough, as well as being someone you can have fun with and enjoy being around. Let's take a look at the friendship between Dani and Amber and see how they are able to work through a challenge in their friendship.

*Dani has been best friends with Amber since middle school. They have always been close, and their families are too; they've gone on vacation together and celebrated holidays together. They have different friend groups—Dani plays soccer and spends a lot of time with her teammates and Amber is involved in a lot of school clubs and is part of the student body government. Occasionally, they will have disagreements and differences in opinions about things, but they've rarely had any real drama.*

*Recently, Amber texted Dani and told her that her feelings were hurt after not being invited to the movies with Dani and some of her other friends. Dani was understanding and felt bad that Amber felt left out, but also explained that sometimes her teammates like to do things together just as a team. While the conversation was a little awkward and uncomfortable, both Amber and Dani were able to talk it out and move on.*

The thing about friendships, like Dani and Amber's, is that sometimes they change over time. As you get older, you might notice yourself drifting from friends that you were pretty close to in the past or have known for a long time. You might also start to reevaluate some of your friendships, if they're changing in ways you're not sure you're comfortable with. For instance, you might find you need to have hard conversations with some of your friends if you don't feel heard and supported by them in the ways you want to be heard and supported.

Friendships—like all relationships—aren't perfect and eternal. They're things we have to negotiate—and things we *can* negotiate, if we know how to assert ourselves and communicate clearly about what we see happening in our friendships, and what we want for them.

Still, in the end, you might decide that some of your friends are just not the kinds of people you want to—or can—keep close. This is normal and all part of your journey as you begin to discover who you are and what's important to you—just as the people around you are discovering who they are and what's important to them.

While Dani and Amber were able to work through the hurt feelings in the example above, let's see how their friendship may change as they encounter a new obstacle.

*A few weeks ago, Dani started talking to a new guy, Gavin, who's in one of her classes. He's really funny and has been flirting with Dani, and asked for her number. Right after Dani and Gavin started texting, Dani found out that*

*Amber was messaging him on social media. Dani asked Amber about it and she admitted that they had messaged. Amber apologized and explained that she didn't think that Dani and Gavin were "really" talking. Dani was annoyed with Amber, but also values their friendship and isn't sure that a guy is worth throwing it all away for.*

Amber crossed a line by starting a conversation with a guy that her best friend just started talking to. She did this secretly, behind Dani's back—which doesn't make her look like a very good friend. And although she apologized, Dani is now questioning the friendship and probably isn't too sure that she can trust Amber.

So, what are Dani's options? Dani could try to repair the relationship. She could express her needs and expectations and give Amber a chance to be a better friend and earn back the trust she's lost. Or, Dani might decide that this friendship is not one that she is happy with; she might choose to end the friendship completely. Who she invites into her life is up to her.

And it's the same for you. While these can be tough decisions, it's important for you to feel comfortable and secure in your relationships.

## EXERCISE: REFLECTING ON YOUR FRIENDSHIPS

How are your friendships right now? It can be useful to take an inventory of our friendships, to appreciate the connections we have and reflect on the kinds of friendships we want to develop further.

Take a minute to answer the following questions in your journal.
1. Who are some of my closest friends?
2. Why am I close to them? How do they make me feel?
3. Who are some of my friends who are maybe not so close, but are still important to me?
4. What are some things I can do to feel closer to my friends?

As you're answering these questions, you might realize that there are some friendships that don't make you feel as good as you might want to feel. If so, think through the following questions in your journal:

1. Which aspects of these friendships are unsatisfying?
2. Are these friends whom I can talk to? What would I like to say to them? Or are they friendships that maybe need to end?

If you feel unsupported in a given friendship, or maybe even betrayed or wronged by a friend, you should speak up! Tell your friend how you feel. Hopefully you can work it out, if that's what you want.

If you want to end a friendship because it makes you feel bad, know that that's okay. You deserve friends who are honest and respectful, and you have a right to make the decisions that are right for you. You just need to make sure you're willing to be honest about your feelings, and responsible for your own actions in a friendship.

·

In light of this, let's take a moment to think about how you're doing as a friend.

## EXERCISE: HOW ARE YOU DOING AS A FRIEND?

In the last exercise, you reflected on the quality of your friendships and how they make you feel. In this reflection, take some time to think about what kind of friend you are. Are you being the kind of friend that you want to be?

Grab your journal and use these questions as a starting point.
1. How do I show my friends that I care about them?
2. When my friends and I have disagreements, how do I typically respond?
3. Is there any friendship that I need to make more time for?
4. Do I ever struggle to keep up friendships when I'm busy with other relationships—for instance, when I'm dating someone or in a romantic relationship? If yes, what are some of the ways I can prioritize my friendships while I'm in a relationship?

Sometimes, for whatever reason, you might not be as good a friend as you would like to be—this happens! What's important to remember is that you have the ability to reflect on your own actions, get back on track if you feel you need to, and focus on being as good a friend to others as you want your friends to be to you.

Part of learning how to handle friendships, and how to build strong ones in which you can be supported and support others, is to learn what to do when drama comes up—when you encounter bullies, or just friends who let their hurt feelings or their worst selves get the best of them.

## Conquer the Drama!

It can be hard to avoid gossip or rumors, fighting between friends, betrayal, or bullying—as much as you might want (and try) to. You could be minding your own business, living your life, and focusing on your own relationships—and still, sometimes the drama seems to find you.

It's not uncommon for teen girls to feel insecure and to compare themselves to others. Occasionally, they might say and do mean things, perhaps because of their own insecurities or to make themselves feel better. But that doesn't make bullying okay or excuse the "mean girl" attitude—in others or in yourself.

Let's take a look at Tamara's experience to see how she handles it.

> Over the summer, Tamara started talking to this guy, Raj. Tamara met Raj at a party and soon after, he asked her out. She really likes him, and he met her family too; things have been going well.
>
> But a few weeks ago, his ex, Abby, started rumors on social media about Tamara, telling other people that Tamara's a "slut." Tamara has started getting harassing messages from unknown accounts too. When it was just Abby's posts she had to worry about, Tamara felt a little uncomfortable, but now she feels like she

*can't go to school without worrying about what other people are saying about her or what messages she might get next.*

*Her friend Kiki tells her to just ignore it, especially since none of the rumors are true. And while Tamara knows this and really doesn't want it to bother her, it still does.*

Tamara is in an exciting new relationship but isn't able to really enjoy it because of all the cyberbullying. She hasn't done anything wrong, but she's starting to feel insecure and is worrying about what other people might think of her. Her friend is trying to be supportive and encouraging, but it doesn't really help, because she can't change Tamara's situation.

First, it is not okay for Abby to call Tamara a "slut" or any other slur. Calling *anyone* names is never acceptable—regardless of the situation. And nobody should ever feel ashamed or guilty about their sexuality, whether for the choices they have made or the situations they have experienced.

Slurs like "slut" are used to shame girls and women. Unfortunately, it can be pretty common for people to use these kinds of slurs with each other at school or online, to shame others for their behavior. It's sad to see—but what we need to do is support one another and build each other up, not tear each other down! And again, no one should be made to feel guilty or ashamed for their sexuality or any other aspect of their character or behavior.

This is why having positive and meaningful friendships matters. You need friends like Kiki to help you see when the things you're going through are unfair, and to be your cheerleader—people who'll listen to you, provide reassurance when you need it, and remind you of how important you are.

Second, with all of the different social media platforms available to us, anything and everything can be made public. Bullying has become so much more widespread and harder to escape. It can be difficult to ignore negative comments, rumors, and drama, and it can take a huge toll on your self-esteem and mental health—or even make you feel unsafe.

Based on what we know, what could Tamara do? She could talk to Abby directly and stand up for herself. She could tell her to stop posting about her or messaging her. She could block Abby and her friends and the fake accounts on social media, or even report these accounts to the social media platform. And if this is going on in school, she could report this bullying (because it *is* bullying) to the school administrators.

If she needs to, Tamara could also talk to a therapist about what has been happening and how she has been feeling. She could remind herself that her worth is not defined by other people—what they say or what they think. Unless she has her own concerns about her relationship, other people's opinions or judgments are insignificant—especially if they are not her friends or people she trusts.

Most important, she could reflect on the positive friendships in her life and the people who build her up and cheer her on. At the end of the day, that's what matters most.

Bullying is bullying, regardless of whether it's in person or virtually, and it should be addressed. You always have the option to block any accounts that are harassing you online or report them, and to reach out to trusted adults in your life—whatever you need to do to feel safe. You don't have to face this alone.

## EXERCISE: IS IT BULLYING?

Sometimes it can be hard to tell if something is bullying or not. Look at the examples below, consider whether they are bullying or not, and, in your journal, write "yes" or "no" before checking out the answer key.

1. An unknown account messages you on social media threatening that you "go die."
2. People at school spam you with DMs and call you a "bitch."
3. Your friend says, "Those jeans are okay but I liked the other pair better on you."
4. Someone airdrops an inappropriate image to everyone's phone in the whole class.
5. Someone comments on a picture you posted, saying that you're "ugly."

Answer key:
1. Yes, this is bullying. No one should ever threaten or send you aggressive messages online. This should be blocked and reported.
2. Yes, this is bullying. It is never okay for anyone to call you names, even on social media! You can block and report these users at any time.
3. This one isn't bullying. Although it might make you feel a little bad about the outfit you tried on, your friend is just giving you their honest opinion and it doesn't seem mean-spirited.
4. This one is a little tricky because while the image is inappropriate, it does not seem to be directed to anyone in particular. If this image makes you or someone else uncomfortable, know that you can always report it. You can also talk to an adult you trust if you need more guidance or support.
5. Yes, this is bullying. Posting negative comments and criticizing you is bullying, even if you don't think the words are "that bad." Block and report these accounts!

If this happens to you—if you're bullied by someone on social media, or experience this or other types of conflict in real life—remind yourself that other people's words and opinions do not define you or your identity. If you feel unsafe, you can always report and block messages or talk to an adult. Your worth and value are *not* determined by others. In the next exercise, you'll have a chance to learn and practice assertive communication.

## EXERCISE: LEARNING TO ASSERT YOURSELF

We've talked about and will continue to talk about the importance of asserting yourself in situations that make you feel bad or disrespected. As mentioned in this example with Tamara, if she decides to approach Abby, she should speak to her assertively. Assertive communication is an important skill to learn so that you can stand up for yourself, set boundaries, and express your feelings and needs.

When you need to assert yourself, try to use a firm tone of voice—no yelling—and be clear and direct. If you are talking to someone in person, try to face them, make eye contact, and maintain a confident but relaxed body posture.

Here are some examples of assertive statements you could use.
- I know you are hurt and upset but it is not okay that you're spreading rumors about me.
- I don't like when you talk to me that way.

- It is not okay for you to post things about me.
- I am not okay with that.
- Please stop calling me _____.

Try using some of these assertive statements, or come up with some of your own. You could start by practicing this in front of a mirror. Like any skill, it will take some time to feel natural.

It's also important to remember that some people might not be responsive to your assertiveness or change what they are doing; even so, it is an essential skill for you to develop in your process of personal empowerment.

## Finding Balance between Friendships and Dating

When you start dating and pursuing new romantic relationships, it can be difficult to find a healthy balance between spending time with your friends and spending time with your partner—especially when you are really into this new person! But you need your friends too.

So, how do you find that sweet spot? There are some things you can do to make sure that you are nurturing and making time for both your relationship and friendships. Let's take a look at the situation below for ideas.

*Jacky has been with her partner, Garrett, for almost six months now. Jacky is really into Garrett and has been spending more time with him than anyone she has ever dated or talked to.*

*But while Jacky is really happy in this relationship, she's also noticing that she's spending less time with her friends. When she has the option of hanging out with friends or spending time with Garrett, she almost always chooses him.*

*Jacky misses her friends, but also worries about what will happen if she starts to spend less time with Garrett—maybe their relationship won't be as strong as it has been, or Garrett will feel neglected.*

This situation is very common. When you really like someone and enjoy their company, sometimes all you might want to do is be around them. Other times, you might find yourself prioritizing a relationship out of fear and insecurity. You might worry about what could happen if you don't see your partner as frequently. You might ask yourself, "Will they still like me?" or "What if they think I don't care?"

Whatever the reason, it is extremely important for you to continue to do the things you enjoy and to spend time with the people who make you happy outside of the relationship. When we put all of our time and energy into one person, we can start to neglect other meaningful relationships in our lives. Don't forget that your friends will always be there for you, regardless of your relationship status!

So, how could Jacky navigate this dilemma? First, she could check in with herself and reflect on how things are going. She could ask herself why she has been choosing to spend more time with her boyfriend over her friends, or use the skills discussed in Chapter 2 if she is having any unhelpful thoughts. These could include some assumptions Jacky may be making about how open Garrett will be to her hanging out with friends without him sometimes. Most of us know that our romantic partners have other parts of their lives; we don't expect them to be with us all the time!

Jacky might also consider her values—including how important her friendships are to her—and whether she's living up to them. And if she's worried about what will happen with Garrett and her relationship if they spend less time together, she can always talk to him about it, to share some of her fears and ask for reassurance. If Garrett isn't supportive of her spending more time with friends, this could be a red flag that there may be a problem. (We will get into red flags in the next chapter.) But chances are Garrett will be totally open to the conversation.

Some of this might sound a little basic. But it's not uncommon to have a hard time figuring out what the best course of action is when you're stuck between friends and romantic partners who have different needs. In the end, when you're having a difficult time balancing your relationship and your friendships, remind yourself that this is common—especially if this is one of your first serious relationships.

See if you can find some time to check in with yourself, to see your situation clearly and consider—keeping in mind all the factors at play—what you really want to do and why. You can journal, talk to a trusted adult, or even share your thoughts with a therapist. Sometimes it's best just to pause and reflect before acting.

Also, you can always share your feelings and concerns with your friends and partner. You can try one of these conversation-starters if you are unsure of how to initiate this type of conversation.

With your partner:
> I really care about you, but I'm worried that I'm not spending enough time with my friends.
>
> I want to spend time with my friends this weekend, I feel like I haven't seen them outside of school in a while.
>
> I've been wanting to hang out with my friends but have also been worried that you won't like me as much or think I don't care about you. How would you feel if I spend more time with them?

With your friends:
> Hey, I'm sorry I haven't been around as much, I realize I have been spending a lot of time with _____, but I want to change that.

I know I have been bad about texting and hanging out, I promise I will try harder to be a better friend.

I'm sorry I haven't been a good friend lately, I am going to do my best to be better.

Although it may be awkward, it can be so helpful to be up-front, in order to avoid misunderstandings, and to talk about these things before they become bigger issues. You've got this!

## Let's Recap: Friendship

If you're having a difficult time navigating the challenges of friendships and drama, consider this recap.

**Find Good Friends:** As your social circle grows and changes, it's important to know what makes a friendship a good and supportive one. Good friends treat each other with kindness and respect. They are honest and trustworthy. Your good friends won't call you names or make you feel bad about yourself. They're people you can rely on, and people you want to support you. It's important to find these friendships and circles of people who embrace you, celebrate you, and have your back.

**Assert Yourself:** Set those boundaries by speaking up for yourself! You don't have to put up with others' judgment, name-calling, or any behavior that's hurtful to you. You're entitled to healthy relationships with friends and partners alike—you don't have to put up with anything less. If you feel you're in a situation where your boundaries are being tested, check in with yourself and with the realities of your situation. Figure out what needs to change. And do your best to communicate assertively with the people involved in the situation, to get yourself what you need.

**Shaming People Is Not Okay:** It is never okay to shame or judge someone for their sexuality or sexual history (or anything else). Your worth and value go beyond your sexuality, and nobody has the right to make you feel less than because of your sexuality. Similarly, you shouldn't insult others on the basis of what they do with their bodies. It's up to all of us to treat one another with respect and compassion.

# CHAPTER 6

# Loving When It's Healthy and Knowing When It's Not

Dating and relationships can be fun and meaningful. There is something so special and exciting about having a connection with someone, feeling seen, and sharing experiences. At the same time, you may begin to notice that some relationships are not as healthy as others.

"But what's healthy?," you might be thinking. That's a great question. In a healthy relationship, you and your partner trust and respect one another. You feel safe and comfortable sharing your feelings and expressing any concerns. Even in healthy relationships, people have disagreements, but they're able to work through them respectfully. You'll know a relationship is healthy when you're able to make your own decisions; set boundaries around what you are and aren't comfortable doing, and what kind of treatment you'd like to receive; and have your own friendships and activities outside of the relationship.

A lot of teens (and adults) associate unhealthy relationships with physical abuse—a person hitting or being physically aggressive with their partner. But abuse is not always physical; it can sometimes be more subtle. Abuse can include mental and emotional abuse, as well as sexual abuse.

Abuse is also not gender-specific. This means that people of any gender can be abusive and can suffer from abuse. And it can happen at any age, and in all different types of relationships. What's important to remember is that anything that one partner does to intentionally cause another partner physical or emotional pain and assert control is abusive. Similarly, anything in a relationship that repeatedly causes you to feel bad about yourself could be considered unhealthy.

As you begin or continue to date and enter new relationships, pay attention to how you're feeling. Do you feel seen and understood? Do you feel like your partner or the person you are dating treats you with kindness? Does your partner respect your values and what you have to say? And, most important, do you feel safe? Remember: You matter and are deserving of a relationship that is healthy and supportive.

In this chapter, we'll begin by looking at what you've learned from the relationships of the adults in your life, which for many of us serve as models for the relationships we go on to have. Then, we'll look at what unhealthy behavior in relationships looks like, and ways you can assess your romantic relationships—especially if you sense that they could be unhealthy in some way. Finally, we'll explore what you can do if a relationship is ever less than healthy.

## EXERCISE: LEARNING FROM ADULT RELATIONSHIPS

Take a moment to think about what kinds of models for relationships you've had from your parents or caregivers. Sometimes people will copy the actions of their parents/caregivers (knowingly or unknowingly), or find themselves in similar relationships. Those relationships, up until now, may have been your model of what a romantic relationship looks like, and they may impact how you view and understand relationships today.

Here are some questions to guide your reflection:

1. Did the adult relationships or marriages that you observed growing up—whether that of your parents or other friends or family members—feel positive, negative, or a little of both?
2. Did any of these relationships seem healthy? If so, why?
3. Did any of these relationships seem unhealthy or abusive? If so, why?
4. What are some of the things you liked and did not like about those relationships?

5. Is there anything that you would like to do differently from what you saw in those relationships?

What does this reflection bring up for you? Do you notice any patterns or similarities between your relationships and your family's?

Let's look at what Keisha learned from comparing her relationships to her family's.

*Keisha has been in a few relationships. She's noticed that some of the same things that happened in her family's relationships were happening in her own relationships. She'd had partners who made her happy, like her uncle made her aunt happy. But she also recognized that in a couple of her past relationships, she tended to put herself and her own desires second to her partner's, the way her mom sometimes does with her dad.*

*This insight made Keisha realize that she wants to learn how to be more open and assertive about her own needs in her future relationships, rather than assuming her partner's needs should come first.*

While it can be helpful to reflect on the relationships you've been around, in order to understand your own behavior or expectations, remember that you get to determine the future course of your own relationships.

This also goes for your partner or someone you're dating. A person's upbringing can help you understand them and how they act in relationships. However, it does not excuse abusive or unhealthy behaviors.

How can we figure out if another person's behavior is unhealthy or abusive? It can sometimes be challenging—but there are ways. Let's look at some of them now.

## Being in Tune with Yourself and Your Relationship

It can sometimes be challenging to figure out if the action or behavior of another person is unhealthy or abusive. Most of us form our understanding of relationships from what we observed growing up—the relationships between our parents/caregivers, relationships that our friends are in, and the relationships that we see on TV. So, if you have parents that are always fighting and calling each other names, it could seem "normal" for partners to put each other down. However, only YOU get to determine if a relationship makes you feel good or not. Trust your gut and tune in to how you are feeling.

Check out Bella's experience, to see how she navigates a potentially unhealthy situation with her partner.

*Bella has been with her girlfriend, Kat, for a little over two months now. Kat has recently started to get jealous and is always asking her who she's with. At first, Bella thought it was kind of cute, because it showed that Kat cared about her. But Kat also never believes Bella when she tells her that her friends are just friends, or tries to reassure her that she doesn't have romantic feelings for anyone else.*

*Recently, things came to a head when Kat messaged Bella after Bella posted about a fun night out at a movie with friends—accusing Bella of doing something wrong and trying to make her feel like a bad girlfriend because she was spending time with other girls, without Kat being there too. It's as though Kat doesn't trust Bella to be out of her sight, in a way that makes Bella feel exhausted and disrespected.*

This is an example of someone trying to *control* their partner, as well as using guilt and shame to make them feel bad about themselves. Kat is checking Bella's social media as a way to keep track of her. Kat may be feeling jealous or insecure, but it is *not* okay for her to tell Bella where she can go and who she can spend time with. In a healthy relationship, each partner should be able to hang out with their friends and trust each other, even if the other person is not around. Bella should be able to decide how she spends her time without being scared that Kat will get mad or break up with her.

Partners should also be able to manage their own feelings—rather than let their feelings drive them to behave in ways that are abusive and controlling, as Kat's doing. If Kat feels insecure, she needs to look at the reality of the situation (rather than just what she fears), be honest with Bella about how she feels, and trust that Bella will be a responsible partner, rather than assuming the worst and trying to control where Bella goes and what she does.

It's not uncommon to be in Bella's position. Many of us would justify the type of behavior Kat's engaging in as an act of love. Sometimes a partner will try to gain control by keeping someone away from their friends and family—so that *they* become their partner's top priority. And while this controlling behavior might seem harmless because it is somewhat subtle, it can be a sign of an unhealthy relationship, even abuse. Again, like we said earlier, a behavior does not have to be physically violent to be unhealthy or abusive.

If you have ever been in a similar situation or if you experience something like this in the future, trust your gut, remember your rights, and do whatever you need to do to be happy and feel safe. You should never feel controlled, threatened, or intimidated by your partner; nor should you have to justify yourself or explain to your partner about what you are doing or who you are spending time with, just because they might be uncomfortable or jealous. You deserve someone who treats you with kindness and respect and makes you feel *good* about yourself;

and you can communicate these expectations to your partner.

Going back to the situation between Bella and Kat, Bella can use assertive communication to tell Kat that what she's doing is not okay, and that Bella expects Kat to be able to manage her own feelings rather than not trusting Bella because of her own fears. She can also emphasize the importance of her friendships and having time to herself outside of the relationship.

## EXERCISE: ASSESS YOUR RELATIONSHIP

How can you tell if your relationship is unhealthy or you're being abused? Unfortunately, it's not black and white. A good rule of thumb is that if you ever feel uncomfortable or your gut is telling you that something is not right or okay in your relationship, you should think about how the relationship makes you feel. Some questions to ask yourself and journal about in these moments are:

- Do you have a sense of freedom in your relationship?
- Do you feel like you get to make your own choices?
- Do you feel good about yourself in the relationship and when you're with your partner?
- Do you always feel safe?

Do you feel supported by your partner?
Do they respect your decisions?
Do you feel like you can express how you feel?
Do you communicate in a healthy way?
Do you feel like you can change your mind?
Can you stand up for yourself?
Does your partner treat you with kindness and respect?

If you answer "no" to even one of these questions, remind yourself of your rights—what you are entitled to in *every* relationship. You have the right to be treated with respect, to feel supported and safe, to be yourself, to have freedom outside of your relationship, and, most important, to be *happy*. All of us have these rights, and you can assert them at any time!

## Detecting Unhealthy Behaviors or Subtle Abuse

Some abusive behaviors are harder to see than others. Like in the example above, a partner questioning you or telling you who you can and cannot see might not seem unhealthy or abusive at first, but if you pay close attention to how you *feel*, you might start to think differently.

Similarly, abusive language can also be tricky to detect and may not seem "that bad" if it is not obviously offensive. But your partner does not need to use foul language for it to be abusive. The abuse isn't always apparent from someone's outward actions, but rather can come to light by looking at how the action made you feel or the effect it had on your life and mental health.

Let's have a look at this next conversation between Caila and Jesse.

> Caila has been with her boyfriend, Jesse, for over a year. They have been arguing a lot and, since she started a job at a restaurant four months ago, he is upset with her for working so much and not having enough time for him. He has been telling her that she is selfish and shallow, because she is trying to make money and bought herself some nice things since she started working. Caila doesn't think that she's doing anything wrong, but is beginning to question herself. It makes her feel bad when Jesse is rude to her. She isn't sure if how he is acting is unhealthy or not.
>
> Last night, when Caila told Jesse she'd need to work until 8p.m., not 6p.m., to cover for a coworker who had to leave her own shift early, Jesse called her "selfish," even after Caila explained the situation. "I always make time for you," he added. "You never make time for me. Maybe you should think about what's really important to you and if you even have time for us."

Jesse does not seem to respect or support Caila's decision to start working, or her freedom and interests outside of their relationship. He is using putdowns, making accusations, and not taking responsibility for his own feelings or actions. Jesse is most likely behaving unfairly toward Caila because of his own insecurities, and his inability to deal with a change in the relationship flexibly. And although this meanness may be unintentional, it is still unhealthy.

Another thing to consider is that Jesse has acted like this before. This isn't a one-time thing and, instead, looks like it could be a pattern. Caila is also starting to feel bad about herself because of the fighting, which is a *huge* red flag and another indicator that this relationship may not be healthy.

In a healthy relationship, your partner should be supportive and respectful of your decisions. Even if they don't agree with your decisions, they should still respect your ability to make decisions outside of the relationship. Your partner should not call you names or put you down (and yes, "selfish" *is* an unkind word). Your partner should never punish you or force you to make a decision that doesn't feel good to you. Most important, your relationship should *never* make you feel bad about yourself. Relationships, although sometimes messy and complicated, are meant to be positive, uplifting and motivating.

So, what could Caila do? It's great that she's aware that something doesn't feel right and also notices that her relationship is making her feel bad. Similar to Bella in the previous example,

Caila could first try to have a conversation with Jesse and set limits with him, being clear about what *is* and *is not* okay moving forward. If Jesse is able to take responsibility for his unhealthy behavior and make necessary changes, great!

However, if Jesse is unable to take accountability and change, or Caila feels like this relationship is more harmful than beneficial, she can make the decision to end it. She doesn't have to sacrifice her happiness and self-worth. If the relationship makes her feel bad, it's her right to make a decision that's best for her.

If you ever find yourself in a relationship like this one, remember to check in with yourself. Ask yourself, "How do I feel in this relationship?" This question might sound simple enough, but we know that answering it may be a little confusing and complicated, especially when you have strong feelings for this person. When you truly love someone or care deeply for them, it can be hard to acknowledge unhealthy patterns or abuse. But it IS possible that the person you feel you love the most is a person who's hurting you. So, you have to trust and be direct with yourself. If you are in a relationship that is harmful to you in any way, stand up for yourself and be your own protector.

Ending a relationship with someone you care about is hard; there is no question about it. But you will feel so much better in the long run if you end a relationship with a partner who makes you feel bad about yourself. Never forget that you deserve a partner who lifts you up and makes you feel good!

Up until now, we've been looking at relationships that are perhaps more subtly than explicitly abusive. The ways Kat and Jesse were behaving toward Bella and Caila aren't okay. But both Kat and Jesse may have been driven by insecurity, rather than being intentionally hurtful.

There are also forms of abusive behavior that are more clearly abusive. Before we close this chapter, let's look at the signs of a relationship that's explicitly abusive, so you know to recognize those relationships—and how to handle them.

## EXERCISE: CHECKING FOR RED FLAGS

Take some time to review these "red flags" below, to understand what it looks like when a relationship is abusive.

It may be intense to read through these lists. Please know that they're meant to give you the tools you need to feel empowered as you date and navigate relationships. And know that you can always take breaks if you need to, as you read. You can also find friends, loved ones, and trusted adults to talk to about anything you need to work through or share.

It may be a red flag of *psychological abuse* when your partner:

- Asks to check your phone and/or demands your passwords
- Does not want you to spend time with friends or family, or guilts you when you do
- Gets mad when you make plans that don't involve them or asks you to cancel plans for them
- Tells you what and what not to wear
- Gets upset when you don't text back right away
- Needs to know where you are and who you are with at all times

It may be a red flag of *emotional abuse* when your partner:
- Calls you names (i.e. "bitch," "slut," "pathetic," "ugly," "lazy," "dumb")
- Puts you down or criticizes you (i.e. "You should lose weight," "You are a bad girlfriend," "You can't do anything right!")
- Makes accusations or blames you for things that are not your fault or outside of your control (i.e. "It's your fault I'm failing all of my classes," "It's your fault I got upset and yelled at you")
- Makes threats (i.e. "I'm going to kill you," "You'll wish you never did that")
- Blackmails you (i.e. "If you break up with me I will text everyone that picture I have of you")

It may be a red flag of *sexual abuse* when your partner:
- Pressures you or guilts you to have sex or do things you are uncomfortable doing
- Has sex with you without your consent
- Pressures you to send them nudes or engage in sexting
- Exploits you (i.e. has you have sex or intercourse with other people for their own gain, distributes explicit pictures of you to others)

It may be a red flag of *physical abuse* when your partner:
- Uses any physical force to cause you pain (pushing, slapping, hitting, punching, choking, shaking)
- Uses any physical gesture to intimidate you and make you feel unsafe
- Tries to corner you or block you from leaving
- Throws things at you

We understand that it may be a lot to consider all of this. But being equipped with this knowledge can help you gauge whether a relationship is healthy or not and prevent abuse. In the end, the more familiar you are with these red flags, the more confidence you will have to trust your gut and leave a relationship if it feels even the least bit abusive or unhealthy. Come back to these red flags at any stage of a relationship if you're ever feeling unsure about what you're experiencing and whether it's problematic.

## Recognizing and Responding to Abuse

As we've discussed, abuse can look different from relationship to relationship, and it doesn't have to be physical for the relationship to be abusive. Our hope is that through this book and ongoing self-reflection, as you continue to date and have relationships, you'll feel empowered to make decisions and navigate relationships while knowing and protecting your rights and prioritizing your safety.

At the same time, it can help to get a sense of what it looks like when a relationship is clearly abusive, and what to do. Let's take a look at Amber's story.

*Amber has been talking to a guy, Max, for a few weeks. He has taken her on nice dates and has made her feel pretty special. But after about three weeks of talking, and after he asked her to be his girlfriend, he began changing. He started getting mad when she didn't respond to his texts right away, and one night, at a party, he pushed her because he saw her in a group of people, standing next to another guy. Amber fell down and he walked away.*

*Until now, Amber has never been pushed by anyone she has dated. She never thought something like this could happen to her. She wonders if it's her fault or if there was anything she could have done differently to keep it from happening.*

Though this was the first time Max pushed her, Amber had been noticing other warning signs, including Max being controlling and possessive. She may have brushed these things off before, but is now becoming more worried.

*Max apologized to Amber afterward, and now she's considering letting it go. But when she shared the incident with her friend Missy, Missy told her it doesn't matter that Max apologized. The fact that he pushed her, and that he's been controlling and possessive before—these are all bad signs. Missy tells Amber that she'll be better off if she breaks up with Max before things get worse. Max clearly doesn't know how to treat his partners well.*

Unfortunately, this does happen. An abuser will hurt their partner and then apologize and try to convince them that it was a mistake or a one-time thing. But even if they apologize and promise you that they will never do it again, it is *not okay*. It is *never* okay for someone to hurt their partner. Whether it's hitting, punching, throwing something, or pushing, this is all *abuse*. And often—especially when the abusive behavior is part of a pattern, as with Max—it never gets better and often gets worse.

Physical abuse is almost never a one-time thing. Any act of violence is an effort to control you and have power over you. It doesn't matter if you "made them upset" or "started it"—which are things you might hear someone say as explanations or justifications for their abusive behavior. The reality is that we are all responsible for our own behavior, and nothing you say or do is justification for your partner abusing you.

When we're upset with others, we have a responsibility to deal with that upset in a way that's mature and respectful, while still getting our needs met—for example, by having a calm and honest conversation. If someone chooses to respond with abusive behavior instead, it's never okay. You shouldn't have to suffer through it.

Of course, a lot of people struggle with this—with being able to recognize abuse for what it is and respond in a way that allows them to truly protect themselves. It's hard to end a relationship that you are committed to or leave a person you are in love with. And sometimes abusers can be manipulative and use other tactics to get you to stay in the relationship, which can make it that much harder and more confusing.

Below are common tactics used by abusive partners to preserve a relationship in which they abuse:

**Love bombing:** Love bombing often occurs shortly after the abuse. The abuser will start apologizing, showering their partner with love and affection, and making grand gestures (perhaps giving you compliments and gifts). Often, they will make promises like "I will never do that again" to get you to stay. Typically, this is part of a cycle in which the abuse happens, it's followed by apologies and affection, and then another abusive incident occurs.

**Gaslighting:** Gaslighting is a tactic used to minimize the abuse or even blame the victim for the abuse. They might say something like "You made me hit you" or "It's your fault I got so upset," or deny the abuse completely. This tactic is usually used to make you second-guess yourself and question your feelings and judgment.

Regardless of what the abuser says or does, there is no excuse or good explanation for *any type* of abuse. You are worthy of respect, and anyone who makes you feel otherwise is not deserving of your time, energy, or love. And even if you are in a relationship where "when it's good, it's really good, and when it's bad, it's really bad," if there is any type of abuse happening, the "good" should never justify the "bad." You don't ever deserve bad.

If you have been in a situation like this before, you didn't deserve it. Did you hear that? It was *never* your fault. We live in a culture and society that sometimes excuses abusive or unhealthy behaviors, but you *do not* have to tolerate abuse. You do not have to accept it.

So, knowing all of this, what should Amber do? She should get help and end this relationship. There is no excuse for Max's behavior. And if Amber simply excuses the behavior, chances are it will happen again. If she is having a hard time ending it or not sure that she wants to, she should talk it out with someone. If she feels unsafe at any time, she can talk to a trusted adult or mental health professional, or call 911 for immediate help.

And what can *you* do if you experience blatant abuse? Leave the relationship. It is *that simple*. Nobody should ever put hands on you, or threaten you viciously, or pressure you to do things you're uncomfortable doing without respect for your rights and your consent. Ever.

If you're ever in this position, and you feel too scared to end the relationship, talk to a trusted adult or professional who can help you make a plan to leave, and get you the support you need. It's not always easy to do this. But it's also true that it will only get harder the longer you stay. And there are *so many* resources and services out there to help people get out and heal from these relationships. In the back of the book you can find the Power and Control Wheel and Equality Wheel, which will show you the different types of abuse and the rights everyone has in a relationship. You can use both of these tools to help you determine the health of your relationship. We'll also walk you through the steps of making a relationship exit plan in the next section.

## *EXERCISE: PREPARING TO LEAVE AN UNHEALTHY RELATIONSHIP*

While we hope that you never find yourself in a dangerous or unsafe situation with a partner, we want you to be prepared in case you do. This is especially important because when your safety's threatened, it's not always easy to "just leave." In these more serious cases, it's important and recommended to create a plan of action and inform a trusted adult. You can use the following outline, along with the sample answers we've provided, to get you started with making preparations of your own.

1. In your journal, write down the names and phone numbers of trusted adults that you can talk or reach out to.
2. Emergency numbers and resources:
    911
    24/7 crisis line 1-800-273-TALK (8255)
3. Write down the places where you feel safe, such as:
    School
    Home
    Library
4. Things to increase safety:

Inform teachers/school administrators, parents, other trusted adults
Change phone number
File a restraining order
Block partner on social media
Connect with a therapist/counselor

Again, dating and romantic relationships can be fun and meaningful. For many of us, these are among the most meaningful relationships we'll have. That's what makes it crucial to know what it can look like when an intimate relationship may be problematic, or even abusive, and what to do about it. This is because when you love or care about someone intensely, it can be hard to leave, even when it's unhealthy. But when you go into relationships knowing what you deserve—a healthy relationship in which you're supported, able to speak and be heard, able to work through disagreements respectfully, and to have your own life—you'll feel more empowered to advocate for yourself. Healthy, respectful love is an experience we all deserve.

## Let's Recap: Relationship Health and Safety

Being in a healthy and safe relationship is your right, but sometimes it can be difficult to detect abuse or know whether or not a relationship is unhealthy. So, as you date and pursue relationships, check in with yourself. If any behavior or situation makes you feel uneasy, insecure, or unsafe, you can always opt out. Remember to trust your gut! And you can always come back to this recap at any time or stage in a relationship for guidance.

**Learned Behaviors:** It's common for teens to repeat or mimic the actions or behaviors of their parents or caregivers or find themselves in similar relationships. Everything that you may have seen in those adult relationships growing up could have impacted how you view and understand relationships today. But, regardless of the relationships that you grew up around, remember that you get to determine the course of your own relationship and what feels good and safe to you.

**Abuse Is Abuse:** Abuse is any type of action or behavior that asserts *power and control* over another person. Abuse can be verbal, psychological, sexual, and physical. Nobody deserves to be abused. And if you experience abuse, it's never your fault. It should never happen, and you can choose to leave a relationship in which there's been abuse at any time.

**You Have Rights:** Remember that you have rights in every single relationship. You have the right to be treated with respect, to feel supported and safe, to be yourself, to have freedom outside of your relationship, and, most important, to be *happy*. If someone does not respect these rights, you do not have to stick around! And remember, more resources and information are available at the end of this book, including the Power and Control Wheel and Equality Wheel.

# CHAPTER 7

# Online Love Doesn't Feel Virtual

Sometimes adults dismiss online relationships as bad, unrealistic, and even dangerous. But we know it's not always like that! People can meet in all kinds of ways and places. The Internet has given us awesome opportunities to connect with people all over the world. And one day you might find yourself interested in a relationship with someone you meet online—or maybe that's already happened. Either way, we're here to help you figure out how to know if someone you meet online is the real deal, and to help you find ways to talk to your parents about online relationships. That way you can communicate with someone online, and potentially have a relationship, but stay safe too.

In this chapter, we'll discuss ways you can keep yourself safe online and when meeting a new partner in real life, and how you can manage expectations, priorities, and screen-time. We'll also consider some of the situations you might run into online that could be unsafe, and things you can do to take precautions and increase your safety.

# What Online Relationships Can Look Like

Online relationships can vary a lot, depending on the situation. Some people might meet online and live in the same city. Others might live really far away from one another and even be in a different time zone.

Any time you're dating someone, whether it's in person or online, it can be challenging to manage your time and communication—but especially so when your relationship is online, because so much of the communication happens on your phone or computer and you both have to juggle your different schedules and plans. It can be helpful to talk about each of your expectations for how much time you spend with each other, and with your friends or other activities. Let's look at Cece's experience communicating with her partner, Drake.

*About a year ago, Cece met her boyfriend, Drake, on social media, in the comments section of a band they both like. They both commented on the same post and so Drake DM'd her and they started talking. They've never met in person, because he lives in another state, but they're hoping to meet up once they both graduate from high school. For now, they FaceTime—and their parents have even talked to each other! Recently, though, Cece's parents have been getting mad at her because they think she spends too much time on her phone talking to him and not enough time on everything else.*

Here, it's clear that Cece started her long-distance relationship with Drake in a way that's safe and healthy. They speak via FaceTime, so each of them knows that the other person really is who they claim to be—the same age, that they live where they claim to, and so on. And their families have met. Both Cece and Drake know about each other's families and real lives.

All of these things are great! They also reveal the guidelines you'll want to follow if you meet someone online that you might be interested in romantically.

- First make sure that they are who they say they are and that you're not at risk of being "catfished" (when people post fake pictures and account information).
- Keep your parents or caregivers in the loop, especially since they're going to be wondering who you're talking to all the time (and they'll probably find out anyway). It may feel like you're giving up privacy this way, especially when a relationship is new and you're still figuring things out—but ultimately, it'll help keep you safe.
- If you notice that you're neglecting other parts of your life to focus on the relationship,

have a conversation with your partner so that you can take care of what's important and still make time for each other.

Right now, it seems like Cece might be spending a little *too* much time focusing on Drake, and it's starting to cause problems. It sounds like Cece needs to have a conversation with him about how much and how often they talk. Maybe they can agree that they'll talk once she finishes her homework and has dinner with her family. That way they can talk uninterrupted later, but she's still making time for other things that are important.

Cece is learning how to communicate with Drake about managing both of their priorities and expectations. This is a skill that's crucial to learn in relationships of all kinds, whether online or in person.

## EXERCISE: MANAGING PRIORITIES AND EXPECTATIONS IN A RELATIONSHIP

We all have different parts of our lives that are important to us. Family, friends, school, sleep, work, and extracurricular activities are just a few examples of different parts of our lives that we spend time on. Grab a piece of paper and make a list of the different parts of your life that are important to you.

Next, draw a big circle. Make a pie chart, which might look something like this:

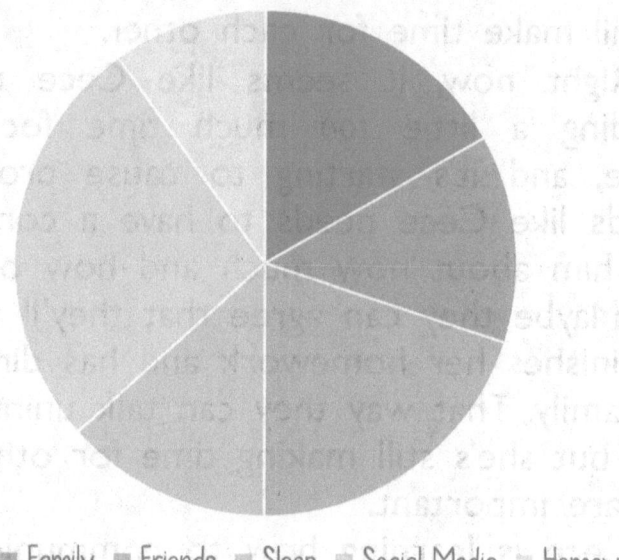

■ School  ■ Family  ■ Friends  ■ Sleep  ■ Social Media  ■ Homework

Take the examples you wrote on your list and add them into the pie chart. If you are in a relationship, include that time too. Be honest with yourself about how much time you're spending on each item!

Now sit back and take a look at your chart. Are there areas that you need to spend a bit more time on? Are you spending too much time on certain things? If you need to make changes in order to prioritize different parts of your life, use this visual aid to guide you. In a healthy relationship, each partner will communicate and understand when one or both of you need to prioritize different parts of your lives.

In addition to managing time, expectations, and communication, people in online relationships are sometimes considering whether or not to meet up in person. The next section will guide you through options for meeting up with someone you've met online, and how to do that safely.

## Deciding to Meet Up

Sometimes in an online relationship, the person might live really far away from you, and so it's not possible to meet up in person. Other times, they might live close to you and you might decide that you want to meet them. This can be a little tricky! No matter how old you are, meeting up with someone you met online can be a risk. It can be hard to know if the person is really who they say they are, or what their intentions might be. The person could be totally nice and normal—but there's a possibility that's not the case and it could be unsafe.

Let's look at Bianca's experience and how she decided if she wanted to meet Patrick in person.

*Bianca was looking at her friend's social media stories and she saw a really cute guy named Patrick in them. She messaged her friend to ask who he was and the friend ended up giving Patrick her username so they could talk. It turned out that he went to a high school near hers.*

*They've been messaging for a few weeks now and he wants to meet up at a movie on Friday with friends. Bianca is excited to meet him but she doesn't think her parents are going to let her go. She doesn't know what to tell him.*

In this case, Patrick isn't a complete stranger, because Bianca's friend knows him. But Bianca still doesn't really know much about him. She told him that she needs to check with her mom as to whether she can meet him, which is good because she's being honest with him and with her mom. It's also great that the proposed meeting is in a public place with their friends.

In this situation, Bianca could explain to her mom how she "met" Patrick and what she knows about him so far. She could tell her mom about her proposed plan (where, when, with whom). We don't know if her mom will let her go or be okay with it, but it's important to be clear with her either way.

If you're in a situation like this, make sure to look at all the angles. Safety comes first and you'll want to come up with a plan to keep yourself safe. We know it might sound excessive, but people aren't always who they seem to be and you have to keep that in mind. The best option is to let the adults in your life know what's going on so that they can help to make sure you're safe; that way you don't have to keep secrets either. It's best if you meet up with a new person in a group in a public place, rather than alone. Also, don't accept a ride from someone you've never met before—consider a safer transportation option. Finally, keep in mind the time of day that you are meeting with this person and who you can call if you need help.

Of course, it might feel hard to know how to talk openly to an adult or anyone about someone you've met online, even as you prepare to meet that person in real life. In the next exercise, you'll learn ways to communicate about this with a parent or guardian.

## EXERCISE: COMMUNICATING WITH YOUR PARENTS AND GUARDIANS

Depending on the type of relationship you have with your parent or guardian, it might feel easy to bring up the topic of dating, or it could feel awkward and nerve-wracking. Every family is unique when it comes to communication styles, as well as rules and expectations about cell phones, social media, and dating. Try to keep the line of communication open and remember that any rules that your caregivers have for you are meant to keep you safe. Here are some examples of conversation-starters that you could use:

1. Hey Mom, can we talk about something when you're free? This guy I know through

a friend asked me out. We haven't met before, but we're thinking about going to a movie as a group on Friday, and I would meet him there.
2. Tía, how old were you when you started dating? I met someone cool online and we talk a lot but they live in Canada.
3. Dad, this guy I've been talking to wants to go to the mall with me, but I know you probably want to meet him first.
4. I hope you aren't mad, but I've been talking to someone online for a while and we are thinking about meeting up in person. I wanted to be honest with you about it.

Write your own ideas in your journal. Only you can know what feels right for you when it comes to your communication with your parents/guardians. Try to choose a time to talk when everyone is calm and there aren't too many distractions going on. Be as honest as possible, and remember that some parents have a hard time getting comfortable with the idea of their kids getting older and dating—but that doesn't mean you shouldn't talk about it. If your parents have a No Dating rule, have a conversation with them about their concerns and expectations so that you can understand their reasoning. Check in often about how things are going.

# Staying Safe Online

Up to this point, we've been talking about online relationships that go well—where everyone is who they say they are, and parents and caregivers are reasonably open to the relationship. But when it comes to communicating with people on social media and online, it's always important to be careful and to know the risks. It can be really hard to tell who someone is and what their intentions are. Sometimes someone can seem really nice at first, but then that can change.

Let's look at Ellie's experience, when Nolan messaged her on social media.

*A week ago, a guy named Nolan DM'd Ellie and said that he thought she was cute, and he "like"d some pics of her and her friends. He said he used to go to her high school (he recognized the mascot in the background of a pic she posted from a pep rally) and now he works nearby.*

*Nolan seemed nice and pretty cute, and it was fun for Ellie to have someone to talk to, to distract herself when her parents have been fighting. But it's also been a little weird. Nolan sent Ellie a pic of himself with no shirt on at the gym, and he asked her if she'd send him some pics back. He also asked if she wanted to come over and watch a movie, and even offered to pick her up.*

*Ellie doesn't really know him and he's older than her, but she doesn't want to be rude, because he seems nice and he really gets her. She's not sure what to do.*

There are a lot of red flags here! Though Nolan might seem nice, he's doing some pretty sketchy things. Let's look at this a little more closely.

1. He figured out where Ellie goes to school because of a small detail in the pic, which is somewhat unusual behavior.
2. He's an older guy who's DMing high school girls he doesn't know—also a suspicious thing to do.
3. He's sending her shirtless pics, which is inappropriate—Ellie didn't ask for them. And he also wants pictures of her.
4. He wants her to come over to his place, even though they've never met before—which is a strange thing to ask so soon, and not safe!
5. He's offering to drive her—which is a little pushy, and unsafe, because she'd be alone in his car and he'd know where she lives.

Alarm bells should be ringing in Ellie's head, but we know she also wants a distraction because her parents are fighting.

As we've discussed, social media can be fun, but it can also be unsafe. Some platforms ask you to turn your location on, which means people can literally see where you are. And if your profiles aren't private, anyone can see your pics and stories and figure out where you are at that time. Even if your profiles are private or set to friends-only, there are still a lot of people who can see what you post. And unfortunately, there are people out there who use social media to take advantage of others. So it's always safer to turn your location off and to keep your profiles private. This will help you make sure that you and your friends stay safe, so you don't end up in Ellie's position—faced with someone who's behaving in untrustworthy ways and trying to get her to do things she's not sure she wants to do.

So far Ellie hasn't sent Nolan any pics, even though he asked for them. This was a good decision, because it's never a good idea to send pics to someone you don't know. You don't know what their intention is, and once you send them your photo they can do anything they want with it.

In this situation, it sounds like even though Ellie thought Nolan seemed kind of nice and cute, her gut is telling her that it's a little too weird to have an older guy doing the things he's doing, and she'd rather not take this any further. She could tell Nolan that she's not comfortable talking to him anymore and then she could block him. She could also report his account to the social media platform and explain why. Since he knows what high school she goes to, she could tell her parent or someone at school about him if she feels unsafe.

Ellie's a little worried about being rude to Nolan, but at the end of the day she knows her safety is the most important thing, and that it just doesn't feel good to have him asking the things he's asking. You might think that being assertive or setting a boundary is impolite—girls in particular are often raised with the idea that they shouldn't be mean—but it's not! Especially when it comes to your safety. There's a difference between being mean or rude, and setting an assertive boundary with someone. Your personal well-being, safety, and comfort are always more important than how someone perceives you.

If you're ever in a situation like this, here are some ideas about how you could handle it. If you get a message from someone you don't know online, trust your gut. If your gut is telling you that something is uncomfortable or inappropriate, then it probably is. Unfortunately, there are a lot of people online who have not-so-nice intentions when they message you and could be dangerous. Sometimes people aren't even who they say they are! This happens a lot on dating apps, in particular. Remember that dating apps and sexual content apps like OnlyFans are mostly used by people in their twenties and older and aren't designed for teens. There can be a lot of risks for teens who use dating or sexual content apps, so it's better if you don't.

Sometimes predators use the Internet to target younger people, especially women and girls. This may sound intense, like something you can't ever imagine happening to you or anyone you know. But it's worth understanding a little more about what this can look like. Let's take a look at some of the really big red flags to look out for.

## Danger Signs Online

Following are some signs that a person you've met online is chatting with you for reasons that could be exploitative of you. These red flags also apply to someone you might be dating in person, not just online.

1. You meet someone who seems really nice at first, almost like a close friend or even a guardian. They might say really romantic things. Then, that can change and they might start to isolate you from your own friends and family. This helps them gain control.
2. You start dating someone who buys you expensive gifts, like a phone, purse, manicures, etc. Later, they may use these gifts to pressure you into sexual activity.
3. You start dating in person, and they take you to parties or pressure you to use drugs and alcohol.

4. They offer to give you a place to stay or nice meals in exchange for sex. They might try this especially if you don't get along with your parents or family, or are thinking of leaving home and running away, and they know that.
5. Over time, they might start to coerce you or force you into engaging in sexual activity with them or with people they know. They might also try to get you to convince your friends to do it too, by saying that they'll pay you or buy stuff for you and your friends. They can get violent or threaten you if you don't agree.

Again, some of these red flags may sound absolutely inconceivable to you. But this—the possibility that you might meet someone online whose goal is to take advantage of others, exploit, or harm them—is a reality of life, and it's worth knowing about so you can keep yourself and those you know and love safe. For more information on this topic—and how to get help for you or a friend in dealing with any of these issues, if you need it—check the back of the book for resources.

But please also know that we mean to inform you, not just alarm you. And we definitely realize that not everyone online is bad. A lot of people can and do form awesome friendships and relationships with people they meet online!

We just want to make sure that you are safe. In the end, it's important to keep an adult informed about who you talk to online so that they can help you to know if something could be unsafe. And if you notice *any* red flags, don't meet up with the person in question, don't continue the conversation, and report the accounts or incidents if you need to. You got this!

Okay, time to put your knowledge to the test!

## EXERCISE: WHAT WOULD YOU DO?

Below are some sample scenarios of situations you might encounter online. Read through them and think about what you would do in that situation. You can also write the answers down in your journal if you like. We've given you a possible solution for each.

**Possible Unsafe Scenarios**

A random guy sends me a dick pic on social media.
Possible Solution: *Block the user and report the incident.*

My boyfriend, whom I've been talking to online for months, says he wants to send me a gift and he needs my address.

Possible Solution: *Don't share your actual address and consider other options like an e-gift.*

A girl I've been talking to on a fan fiction site says she really likes me and wants to be my girlfriend, but she's never told me her name or age, or shared a photo.
Possible Solution: *Get more information and keep a trusted adult in the loop.*

I keep getting more and more friend requests and messages from random people on my public accounts on social media, and some of them are inappropriate with explicit pictures and sexual messages.
Possible Solution: *Report the inappropriate content and make your account private.*

My friend is using a dating app and she says I should go on too because she keeps meeting older guys who buy her fancy dinners. Sure, she says, some of them are creepy, but most times she thinks it's worth it.
Possible Solution: *Don't go on the app and talk to an adult about what's going on with your friend.*

I entered my phone number when I was trying to buy something online and now I keep getting weird sexual text messages.

Possible Solution: *Block the number and let a parent/guardian know.*

On my social media account, my location is turned on, and this guy who knows my friend messages me and says that he's at the mall too and wants to meet up.
Possible Solution: *Turn your location off and let an adult know if you feel unsafe.*

If you struggled with any of these answers, you can ask a trusted adult for help or to talk things through. These are complicated scenarios, and even adults can struggle to know what to do online or when relationships of any kind get complex. But when you think about how you would handle these situations in advance, it can help you to know what to do if you or a friend are ever in that situation.

## Let's Recap: Online Relationships

We know that not all online relationships are bad and unsafe. We also know that there are some things you need to think about when you're online, so you can have fun and not have to worry. Let's recap some of the chapter's main points to keep in mind when pursuing an online relationship.

**Creating Balance:** When you're in a relationship, it can be hard to balance all the different aspects of your life. We already spend lots of time on our phones and devices, and if your relationship is online too, that means even more screen time! Be clear with your partner and set expectations about how much time you can spend on the relationship.

**Communication:** We know it can be awkward to talk to your parents about who you're dating, but this is especially important when you met someone online. Keep your parents or caregivers in the loop so that they can help make sure you're safe. If you aren't able to talk to your caregivers about it, find a trusted adult, like a friend's parent, that you can talk to about it.

**Safety:** Don't ever tell someone you met online your full name, address, the school you go to, or any other identifying information. They might be a nice person, but just in case they're not, you want to keep yourself safe and not give them a way to find you. If you've received any sexual pictures from someone online, make sure to report it and don't send any back. And don't meet up with anyone you've met online without telling a parent or trusted adult. If someone is harassing you online, or approaching you in ways that feel wrong or unsafe, take screenshots of the messages, block the individual, and talk to a trusted adult if you feel it'd be useful, showing them the screenshots if you need to.

# CHAPTER 8

# Sex, No Sex, or Something Else? Set Your Terms

Now that you have a better idea of who you are and what you deserve in a relationship, it's time for ... *The Talk*. You might have already had the sex talk with someone or taken a sex ed class. Either way, we want to give you the tools and confidence you need to make empowered decisions based on your own personal values.

The decision whether or not to have sex with a partner is a very personal one and can sometimes be complicated! You might be asking yourself when the right time for you may be, or how far you are comfortable going. You might also wonder what to do if your partner is ready but you aren't yet. What if you feel ready for some stuff but not *everything*? We're here to help you figure it all out.

Ultimately, it all comes down to *consent*, or making sure that you're able to give permission to and to get permission from your partners for anything you want to do—and that they do the same for you. Consent means that you and your partners talk about and agree on what you're willing to do before you do it. It's also about you and your partners staying in touch as you're being intimate with each other, to ensure that no one feels like their boundaries are being violated. And it means that you stay in communication with each other afterward, and all through your relationship, to continue negotiating what you feel is right for you.

The reality is, sex isn't always straightforward or predictable. But if you and your partners communicate as clearly as you can, keeping respect for each other and your boundaries in mind, you'll be in good shape. Ultimately, you'll know you're in a safe and healthy relationship when both of you feel comfortable with the stage and pace of the relationship and any sexual activity in it. You'll feel that you both have the ability to talk about what feels right for you, and you'll feel that your partner respects your right to decide what you do or don't want to have happen.

In this chapter, we'll discuss the process of making decisions about sex, how to give and get consent, and what to do if someone you're intimate with doesn't respect your boundaries. It may be a lot to absorb at times, so go as slowly as you need to. And if anything in this chapter makes you uncomfortable or you want to talk about something you read, know that you can check in with trusted adults and use the resources at the back of this book to get extra support.

## Making Decisions about Sex

In a healthy relationship, partners are able to communicate with one another about what they are (or aren't) ready for when it comes to sex, and how they are feeling about it all. Let's take a look at Lyndsay's experience with her boyfriend, Blake.

*Lyndsay has been dating her boyfriend, Blake, for almost a year. They really love each other and Blake is ready to have sex. Lyndsay thinks she might want to have sex with Blake, but she's not sure if she's ready; she's always been taught that she should wait until marriage, or at least until she's older. She's not sure what to do.*

The decision about whether or not to have sex (or do anything intimate with a partner) is a super-personal one. No one can really know when it's right for you except for *you*. And sometimes even then it's hard to figure out! We all have our own backgrounds, beliefs, and personal experiences that affect how we feel about sex. Some people choose to have sex when they're young, some people wait until they're older; some wait for marriage, and some don't even want to have sex at all! Some people want to have sex with people of the same gender, some people want to have sex with people of a different gender, and some people don't have a preference. A big part of getting older is figuring out your values, your boundaries, and what feels right for you. The main thing to remember is your safety and your well-being. *You* have the right to decide whatever is right for *you!* If you know what your values and your limits are, you'll feel confident to handle these kinds of scenarios if you end up in them.

So, getting back to Lyndsay, what should she do? It sounds like Blake wants to have sex and feels like he's ready for that. In Lyndsay's case, she was raised to believe that she should wait to have sex until she is older or married. It sounds like Lyndsay might not be ready, and her gut is telling her that it's not the right time. She could have a conversation about how they're both feeling and set some limits about what she is and isn't okay with doing. Once they talk and agree on some physical boundaries, that should make Lyndsay feel empowered and safe.

What else could Lyndsay do? Well, for one, she could spend some time talking to a trusted adult. You might be rolling your eyes by now about the "talk to a trusted adult" suggestion. And we get it—it can be *super* awkward to talk to an adult about sex. Some people are able to talk to their parents about sex—and if you can, that's great! But we know that's not the case for everyone, so make sure that you find an adult you trust (even better if it's someone who has values that you admire) and get their advice.

It might be uncomfortable at first, but you'll be surprised how much better you feel once you can talk about it.

Conversations like the one Lyndsay will have with Blake about boundaries and consent are always complex—but they can get a little easier when you take time beforehand to clarify what it is you think you want. Let's take a look at the exercise below, to learn about values and decision-making when it comes to sex.

## EXERCISE: IDENTIFYING VALUES AND MAKING DECISIONS ABOUT SEX

Earlier in the book we talked about values (what's important to you) and self-esteem (how you feel about yourself). When you know who you are and what's important to you, it's easier to make decisions, set boundaries, and stand up for yourself when you need to.

So, time to check in with yourself! Grab your journal and answer the following self-reflection questions:

1. What are my partner's values? Or, what values would I want a future partner to have?
2. How open am I with others? What do I feel comfortable sharing with romantic

partners? What do I find it hard to share with romantic partners?
3. What kind of relationship do I want? Do I want a committed relationship that's exclusive (with my partner dating and being sexually active with only me, and vice versa)? Do I want a committed relationship where we wait to be sexually active? Or do I want something else?
4. What are my personal beliefs about sex?
5. Am I comfortable with my body and do I know how it all works when it comes to sex?
6. Are there any non-physical sexy activities that I'm interested in or comfortable with (reading romantic books/fan fiction, talking about sex, watching romantic movies, etc.)?
7. How will I know when I'm ready to have sex with a partner?
8. Under what circumstances would I want to have sex with a partner? For example, would I want to be in a relationship? In love? Married? Something more casual?
9. What am I comfortable doing with my partner? Am I okay with kissing? Touching? Oral sex? Penetrative sex? Anything else?
10. What am I not comfortable doing with my partner?

11. What do I need in order to feel comfortable and safe with my partner?

Dating isn't always straightforward. Sometimes you might lose sight of your values and what you want in a partner or relationship. Remember, you can always come back to these questions if you're feeling unsure and need a reminder.

That said, keep in mind that you don't *need* to have answers to all these questions right now. They're big questions! It may be enough just to start thinking about them. And your answers to these questions could change over the course of your life.

Don't be afraid to reach out to a trusted adult or loved one with anything you might want to talk about. An adult who's open and has your best interests at heart will appreciate you reaching out to them. And it can be helpful not to have to face these intense questions entirely on your own.

## Giving (And Not Giving) Consent

Asking for consent (permission) is an important part of being intimate with someone. And consent doesn't just happen one time; it should happen each and every time. This is important in order for everyone to feel safe and comfortable. Sometimes you might consent to something at one point, but you might change your mind later—and that's okay! Let's take a look at Taylor's experience with their partner, Marissa.

> Taylor has been talking to Marissa for a few weeks, and when they went out last week things got kind of physical. They did some stuff that Taylor hadn't really done before and Taylor ended up feeling kind of awkward. Taylor could tell that Marissa was into it but isn't sure that they want to do that again. But Taylor doesn't want to hurt Marissa's feelings or make her think they're not into her.
>
> Later, when Taylor's friend Juanita asks them about what happened, Taylor admits that while they had fun, they did some stuff that Taylor found kind of awkward. "Well," Juanita says, "just because you already did something doesn't mean you have to do it again. You can always talk to Marissa about it, right?"

Decisions about what you want to do (or not do) with a partner, and who you want to date (or stop dating), are very personal decisions, and the most important thing is your emotional and physical well-being. You can always communicate with your partners, to ensure that you're not pressured into doing something you don't want to do.

Let's see what happened here. It sounds like Taylor and Marissa did something physical, and now Taylor isn't sure if they want to again, because they feel like it was kind of awkward. The great thing is that their friend Juanita reminded Taylor that just because they did something once, doesn't mean that they have to do it again. Sometimes you might be ready, and you try it out and like it—and there's no problem! Other times you might try it out, but realize that you didn't like it. Or you might have second thoughts about whether or not it conflicts with your values. Or maybe it just makes things in the relationship too intense and you realize you might not be ready after all. You might even realize you don't like something right in the middle of trying it out, and decide to stop. All of these things are okay.

It's so important that you learn to value yourself, take yourself seriously, and look out for yourself, while also respecting your partners. When you value yourself, it's easier to know what you want in a relationship, and easier to stick up for yourself—to communicate with whoever you're intimate with about what you're ready or not ready for. And that's what it means to be empowered. That's part of getting older and dating—owning your power to give consent and communicate how you are feeling. And understanding your responsibility to your partners—that when your partners come to you ready to talk about what they might want or not want in a relationship or in a particular encounter, it's your responsibility to listen, communicate with them clearly, and make the decisions that are best for them and for you, with mutual respect and understanding.

Ideally, Taylor will take what they're feeling and Juanita's good advice and make a decision about what they're comfortable with. From there, they can talk to Marissa about what happened, and make sure Marissa understands that Taylor might not want to do what they did again. And ultimately, Taylor will likely feel so much better once they know what they want, and are able to talk to Marissa about it. As for Marissa, her responsibility is to listen and to honor Taylor's feelings and desires, and stay in communication with Taylor as their relationship continues and evolves.

Of course, it's not always this clean-cut. For instance, what if you tried something once and you didn't really like it but your partner did? Or what if you've done something a bunch of times but something changed and now you don't feel like doing it anymore? That's okay too! It doesn't matter how long you've been intimate with a particular person, or how many times you've tried a particular thing before, or if you tried something with someone once and don't want to try it again with another person. You always have the right to change your mind—to decide in a particular moment what does and doesn't feel right to you. In a healthy and loving relationship, you and your partner will be able to talk about what you are okay with, and you'll give and get consent from each other every time.

Let's take a look at the exercise below to learn about consent.

# EXERCISE: COMMUNICATING CONSENT

Asking for consent is an important part of being intimate with someone. When you and your partner are intimate, it's good to check in with each other about the types of things you are doing, and make sure the other person is okay with it. Here's what it sounds like when you or your partner are asking for consent:

Are you okay with this?
Is this okay?
Should I keep going?
Are you sure?
I want to make sure you're comfortable with this.

Write down some ideas of your own! Grab your journal and write down an example of how you can ask your partner for consent.

When two people are having consensual sexual activity, both people are giving consent to one another. Giving consent is a fun part of the experience with your partner, because it means that both of you feel good about what you are doing. Here are some examples of what it looks like to give consent (both verbally and nonverbally):

Yeah! Let's do this!
Smiling
Okay!
Pulling partner closer

Finally! I've been waiting for this!

Enthusiastically returning partner's advances

Write down some of your own! Grab your journal and write your own example of what it sounds like to give consent.

Saying "no" can also be part of the consent conversation. It's important to feel like it's okay to say no if things don't feel right. Sometimes it helps to have a one-liner that you can keep in your back pocket for those times you want to say "no." Check out a few examples below:

I'm not ready yet. I'm still getting to know you.

I am okay with _____, but don't want to do _____.

No, I told you that I am not comfortable with that.

I care about you, but I'm not ready.

I don't think I'm comfortable with that.

I'd feel more comfortable if _____.

Write your own! Grab a journal and write down your own one-liner that you feel comfortable using with your partner or potential partner.

There are also nonverbal clues that indicate a person is saying "no" with their body. This could look like tensing up, turning away, giving no response to advances, crying, or silence, among others. If you or a partner are saying no (whether verbally or nonverbally) during any intimate moments, stop what you are doing and check in with each other to see how you both are feeling.

Giving and asking for consent could feel awkward at first—these can be difficult conversations to have! Through practice you will find it gets easier, and you'll be able to initiate and navigate these conversations with more confidence.

## Responding to Pressure

Sometimes, couples are on the same page about what they're ready to do physically. Other times, one person might be really excited and ready to move things along faster than their partner is ready for. When this happens, couples should communicate using the consent skills that we just discussed. This way, they can make sure that their boundaries are clear.

But sometimes, even when the boundaries are clear, people might experience pressure from a partner to do something that they're not ready to do. This might look like a partner verbally trying to convince you to do something through guilt or manipulation, or maybe even getting frustrated if you say no and making you feel bad. This can be very upsetting and difficult to respond to.

Let's take a look at Ruby's experience, when her boyfriend, Dylan, pressured her to have sex with him.

*Ruby and Dylan have been dating for a couple months. Things have been going well and Ruby really likes him. The only problem is that Dylan really wants to have sex, and Ruby isn't ready yet. Almost every time they start to make out, he asks her if they can have sex. At first, he was sort of silly about it, but recently he's been acting more and more frustrated when Ruby says no. They've had a few arguments about this, but he keeps pressuring her.*

*Dylan feels annoyed that Ruby doesn't want to have sex yet. In his mind, since things are going well and they like each other, why not go for it? Ruby feels bad that she might be disappointing Dylan, but she's also angry with him for pressuring her when she's told him many times that she's not ready.*

In this situation, Ruby has clearly communicated a boundary with Dylan and he is not respecting her boundary. Even though they like each other, this is causing a lot of problems in their relationship, especially because Ruby isn't feeling respected. Just because Dylan wants more out of their physical relationship, that doesn't give him the right to pressure her and get frustrated with her. There is no magic formula for how long it takes a person to feel ready to have sex—it's different for everyone! In a healthy relationship, partners will be able to discuss their comfort level with different sexual activities in a calm and respectful way. If one or both people feel that the physical aspect of the relationship isn't working for them, they can make the choice to end the relationship.

If you're ever dating someone who is pressuring you to do something that you're not comfortable with, have a conversation with that person and make sure they know your limits. If they don't respect your limits, it's time to move on.

A person who cares about you will respect your decision and won't pressure you. Period. Someone who respects you will have no problem waiting until you're ready, and will accept if that's not something that you're willing to do. Or, they'll be honest about the fact that they want something different for the relationship than you do, and you'll be able to move on to find a relationship that's better for you in the long run.

So, get out there and find someone who treats you with respect! And remember, it's okay to put yourself and your desires first. Like Ruby, who felt bad for disappointing Dylan, a lot of us are taught to people-please, to take care of others and not upset them. But your boundaries are valid; in fact, they're the most important thing. It's not "hurting" someone to tell them what you do or don't want. In fact, it's an expression of kindness to yourself and to them—a sign that you value both what they might want *and* what you might want and are ready for.

## What If It Wasn't Your Choice?

Some readers may have had a sexual experience that didn't feel like it was their choice, or that they didn't consent to. This is actually more common than most people realize. If this has happened to you or someone you know, this section will provide more information on what to do and how to get help. Let's take a look at Callie's experience with Bryce below.

*Callie recently had sex with this guy Bryce that she'd been hanging out with. They had talked about sex before and had agreed that all they were comfortable with at that point was making out; they were going to wait until they had been dating longer to have sex. But the last time they hung out, everything just happened so fast and Callie didn't know what to do or how to say no, so she just kind of froze until it was over.*

*So, it happened. Callie felt really bad afterward. In the car driving home, she found herself crying. Now she's not sure what this means. She feels guilty that she didn't stop it. And she doesn't know how to feel about Bryce—who keeps texting her, wanting to know what's up.*

Alright, this one might be tough to talk about. You may have gone through something like this—and if you haven't, someone you know might have. Callie is upset because she and Bryce had sex when she wasn't ready, and Bryce seems confused. You've probably heard people say "no means no," right? Well, actually, sometimes it's really hard to say "no" out loud. Especially if you're scared. Or especially if something bad has happened to you before. But remember, silence doesn't imply consent.

Here's the truth: When someone you are dating has sex with you, but you haven't given consent, this is considered date rape. In other words, it's a form of sexual assault.

This may be hard to hear. And, if you've ever been in a situation where consent was unclear—on either side—this may be hard to even think about. But the truth is that sexual assault and abuse are real issues that impact many people's lives. We're not trying to scare you, but things like this do happen. And many of us who experience it don't talk about it—maybe because we're scared, or ashamed of what might have happened to us, or we feel like it's our fault.

But thanks to movements like #MeToo, people are talking a lot more about sexual assault; they're able to get the understanding, help, and support they deserve, and we're able to learn and educate each other about consent so that no one's boundaries are ever violated.

# Understanding the Freeze Response

The material we're going to discuss in this section is intense. So, as you read, be prepared to take breaks if you need to, and to stop and find someone to talk to if you need support. You might want to read with a pen and your journal handy, so you can make notes about what you read and take your time with it—really absorb it.

Have you heard of the "fight, flight, or freeze" response? When something scary or stressful happens to us, we either fight back, run away, or freeze. For instance, if we're walking on the sidewalk and we see someone coming toward us on a bike super-fast, we might:

1. Put up our hands to try to block that person and minimize the damage (fight response),
2. Scramble to get out of the way (flight response), or
3. Panic, because we're surprised at the sight of the person on the bike and things are happening so fast that we find we're unable to do anything at all (freeze response).

It's no different in the situation Callie was in. She was faced with something she didn't know how to handle, and it made her freeze. When you're in a freeze response, you might feel totally stuck: you can't scream, you can't run, you can't fight, you can't do anything—you're just frozen. That doesn't mean it was Callie's fault. And if it has happened to you, it wasn't your fault either.

What about Bryce? Despite the fact that Callie and Bryce had agreed that they weren't going to have sex, Bryce crossed this boundary. Bryce may not have realized that what they were doing wasn't okay, and now Callie is feeling confused and upset—as well as guilty, because she thinks that she "let it happen." Bryce probably thought Callie was okay with what was happening because she didn't say that she wasn't. But that doesn't mean he should have had sex with her, especially when they had agreed not to. He should have stopped and asked for consent ("Are you okay with this?" or "Are you sure you want to have sex?" or "I know we agreed not to, but now I'm not sure if you want to or not—is this okay?"). Also, he could have been paying attention to some of her nonverbal cues as well. If Callie was tensed up, frozen, and not responding to his advances, this could have been a clue for him that her body was saying no.

So, what can Callie do now? It would be great if she could talk to someone like a parent, school counselor, therapist, or school social worker who knows about the current laws and rights of teens and can help her to figure out what to do next.

It can sometimes be difficult for people to know what to do after a confusing or upsetting sexual experience. Like Callie, people can sometimes find themselves asking questions like "What just happened?" "Was that my fault?" "How do I talk to them about this?" "Was I sexually assaulted?" If you find yourself in a similar situation, try talking to a trusted adult or loved one about what happened, to get some guidance. Talking things through can really help you to sort through your feelings. If, through these conversations, you determine that you were assaulted, there are steps you can take, including being examined by a medical professional, pursuing legal action, and accessing mental health support. You can also check out the resources in the back of the book for more information on this. Don't forget that you deserve to feel safe and that there are people who can help you.

## *EXERCISE: JOURNALING TO COPE*

When something stressful happens to us or someone we care about, it can be very healing to write about it in a private journal. If you are worried about someone reading it, you can tear up the pages afterward, or type it in a document that you delete later. Journaling is helpful because you can write honestly about exactly what's on your mind. You can yell/scream/rage/rant/say whatever you want and no one will judge you!

Try taking 10–20 minutes to write down your feelings about what you're going through. If you need help getting started, here are a few prompts:

Write a nice and loving letter to yourself about what happened.

If you're ready, write a letter (that you won't actually send) to the person(s) who wronged you. Say everything you want to say.

Write about how the experience has affected you: how it shaped you, taught you something, or made you stronger.

Write about ways that you can create safety for yourself, including people, places, objects, music, etc. that comfort you.

These are just a few examples, but feel free to write about whatever you want.

Journaling can be eye-opening, and a good way of processing past experiences. It can also bring up a lot of emotions, so if it becomes too difficult for you, make sure you talk to a loved one for support.

## Let's Recap: Making Decisions about Sex

It can take time to become confident in communicating about consent and making empowered decisions around the subject of sex. Sex is also a very personal thing, and there can be real risk involved if you or your partners aren't as careful as we all should be when it comes to consent, boundaries, and maintaining safety, even as we might want to explore new levels of intimacy with romantic partners. But with everything we've covered in this chapter, you've made a start. Check out this recap to review what we learned in this chapter.

**Know What You Want:** The decision about when to be intimate with someone can be a tough one. Every person has their own unique set of values and once you figure out what yours are, you'll feel more confident in your ability to make a decision that's right for you. Take time to think about what you might want to explore or avoid—knowing that this can and probably will change over the course of your life, and that's okay. Also know that just because you tried something once, that doesn't mean you have to again. You always have the right to determine what should or shouldn't happen to you. That will never change.

**Speak Up—Give Consent, and Get It:** Giving and getting consent is very important when it comes to sex and anything physical. Make sure you can talk to your partner about how you are feeling and what you are comfortable with. You always have the right to be respected and heard. We may not always be able to speak up when it comes to intimacy. Remember the fight, flight, and freeze response, so you can better understand your own reactions and your potential partners' reactions in intimate moments, and ensure that you and everyone you're with feels safe and respected at all times.

**Safety:** You always have the right to feel safe and to be treated with respect by your partner. If you or a friend have experienced a sexual experience that was upsetting or confusing, talk it through with a trusted adult or loved one, to get help and learn what to do next. Journaling about it can also help you to process what happened.

# CHAPTER 9

# Staying Safe During Sex

If and when you and your partner are ready, exploring physical intimacy can be fun and exciting! When you're making the decision to do anything physical with a partner, don't forget about your boundaries—and your health. Sexually transmitted infections (STIs)—also known as sexually transmitted diseases (STDs)—and pregnancy are important things to keep in mind. While some STIs are treatable, others can become more serious, and unintended pregnancy can have a huge impact on your life.

This topic might feel a little scary, but it doesn't have to be! We're here to reassure you that we'll be giving you the facts without the scare tactics you might have experienced in the past. In this chapter, you'll gain knowledge about how to prevent STIs and pregnancy and how to have open and honest conversations with your partner about your sexual health. You'll also learn how to manage situations in which your sexual health has been affected.

# Inform Yourself to Empower Yourself

Before we consider the ways in which sexual activity can impact our health, let's go over the different types of sexual activity. What one person considers to be "having sex" could be different from what another person thinks it is. Different types of sexual interactions include kissing, masturbation, touching one another, oral sex, vaginal sex, and anal sex. These are just some examples of sexual activities that people might engage in, depending on what they are comfortable with. Some of these activities, such as oral, vaginal, or anal sex, are common ways that STIs can be transmitted. Others, such as masturbation or sexual touching, are not common ways of transmitting STIs.

It's important to carefully consider what sexual activity you are comfortable with. Let's take a look at Maya's experience, when deciding whether or not to move forward physically with her boyfriend.

*Jax and Maya have been together for a long time and so far they've only kissed. He's her first boyfriend and she's never done anything other than kissing, but she knows he's had some other girlfriends before and she's not sure how far they've gone. She thinks she might be ready to do more than kiss but she's really freaked out about STIs and getting pregnant.*

*The stuff they showed her in Health class has been stressing her out!*

So, we can understand that Maya feels like she might want to do more than just kiss Jax, but she's really scared of getting an STI or getting pregnant because of what she's learned in her Health class. Some of the info out there about STIs can be really overwhelming.

It seems like at this point in time, Maya is feeling really nervous, so she should wait to move forward with intimacy with Jax until she feels more comfortable. She could also take some time to educate herself about the things she's scared of; knowledge is often the best way to deal with this sort of uncertainty and fear.

If Maya decides later that she's ready, she can talk to Jax about getting tested before they do anything further (more on this later). She could also work on finding ways to speak more openly with Jax about their sexual histories. It seems like Maya is nervous to ask what Jax might have done with past girlfriends—and that's totally understandable. You might find it hard to talk about sex in general, even with your partner. You also may not want to hear about your partner's past partners! But while you may not need to know every detail, it's important to communicate openly and honestly, especially if you're going to be sexually active—for your safety and theirs, and for the strength of your relationship.

If you are considering getting physical with someone, how can you stay safe and avoid getting an STI or getting pregnant? As you might already know from your Health class, sexually transmitted infections can be contracted in a lot of different ways. You can get them from sex, oral sex, anal sex, and even skin-to-skin contact (Centers for Disease Control and Prevention 2021). Pregnancy can occur from vaginal sex. But remember, there are ways to prevent STIs and pregnancy!

Here is a list of the most common ways to prevent STIs and pregnancy:

**Condoms:** Condoms are used on a penis to prevent pregnancy and most STIs.

**Dental Dams:** Dental Dams are used on a vagina to prevent STIs during oral sex.

**Hormonal Birth Control:** Birth control pills, patches, IUDs, implants, and more can be used to help prevent pregnancy. These are just a few of the options that exist to prevent pregnancy; talk to your doctor to learn more. Note that these do not prevent STIs.

**Emergency Contraception:** The "morning after pill" is a medication that is used to prevent pregnancy when taken in the first few days after intercourse has occurred.

**Vaccination:** Shots exist to prevent certain STIs including the Human

Papillomavirus (HPV), Hepatitis A, and Hepatitis B.

**Abstinence:** Abstinence is when someone does not engage in any sexual activity, which removes the risk of pregnancy and STIs.

You might be thinking, "Okay, well, since condoms prevent pregnancy and STIs, if we use a condom then we should be fine, right?" Well, that's a good method, but it's not foolproof. Condoms and dental dams, when used correctly, can be great at helping to prevent STIs, so it's safest to always use one. However, condoms and dental dams only protect the genitals themselves, not the skin around them. So, some STIs such as HPV or herpes can still be contracted even with protection (CDC 2021).

The exercise below will guide you in educating yourself and learning about the different STIs and risks involved in sexual activity, and the prevention and treatment strategies involved with each. It may seem awkward, but it's important, because once you have all the information, you can make a decision about what you're ready for that's truly informed and empowered. And if you decide that you're ready, you and your partner can have conversations about testing and using protection.

# EXERCISE: SEXUAL HEALTH REFLECTION

As you think about your sexual health, ask yourself the following questions. If it helps, you can write down the answers in a notebook, or just think about them.

Do I have a pretty good understanding of STIs and pregnancy?

Are there any specific thoughts or beliefs that I have about STIs and pregnancy?

Are there any fears that I have about being physical with a partner? If so, what are they?

Are there things I can do or steps I can take to help me feel safe and comfortable?

If you don't know all the answers to these questions yet, don't worry. You'll be getting more information as you go and we'll be here to help you along the way. You can also check out the resources in the back of the book for more information on sexually transmitted infections. Also, don't forget that you can talk to a trusted adult or the school nurse for additional information if you need it.

We'll also teach you some strategies for talking to your partners about sexual health, if and when it comes time for that.

# Talking to Your Partner about Sexual Health

Communicating with your partner is one of the most important things that you can do for your sexual health, as well as your sense of safety and security in the relationship. You might feel embarrassed to bring up the topic of protection with a partner, and it's true that it can be a little awkward to talk about sometimes! But remember that getting older and becoming sexually active includes being able to have mature conversations. Let's take a look at Natalia's experience with her boyfriend, Nico.

*Natalia is about to have her one-year anniversary with her boyfriend, Nico, and they both feel like they are ready to have sex and have talked about it. Neither of them has had penetrative sex with anyone, but they both have done some other stuff with people they've dated before. Natalia is thinking that they probably don't have any STIs because they haven't had sex, but she wants them both to get tested before they have sex, just to make sure. She wants to talk to Nico about testing, but she's thinking she will probably just text him since she feels nervous to bring it up in person.*

Natalia's being responsible here—she knows that while she and Nico may be virgins, that doesn't mean they couldn't have an STI (again, you can get an STI in other ways than just having sex), and so she wants both of them to get tested before they do anything. Of course, talking about sex, STIs, and pregnancy prevention can make you feel vulnerable, shy, or embarrassed. This is common—but it's still important to talk about it. If you don't feel like you and the person you want to have sex with can talk about STIs, pregnancy, protection, and testing, then you might not be ready yet.

As for Natalia and Nico, they had already talked about sex and what they're both comfortable with. And though Natalia felt uncomfortable talking about testing and STIs with Nico in person, she still was planning to bring it up over text.

If you're in Natalia's situation, there are things that you can do to feel more confident. If you feel like you and your partner are ready to have a conversation about STIs, testing, and pregnancy prevention, but you're aren't sure what to say, you can write it down, and even practice it out loud. It's always better to have these talks in person if possible, but if you're feeling especially shy or nervous about it, you can start with a text or something similar.

What should you do once you've decided to get tested? If you're able to talk to your parents about this decision, great. If you can't talk to your parents about it or you need to keep it private, you might talk to a trusted adult, school nurse, or school support staff, and see if they can help with anything you might need to do from there.

Whether you have health insurance or not, don't worry. There are many clinics that offer free testing. (You can check out the resources section in the back for more information on how to get confidential testing, or talk to your trusted adult or school nurse or counselor about it. In many US states, there are laws that allow you to seek confidential medical services for sexual health, without anyone else's involvement besides your healthcare providers.)

## EXERCISE: COMMUNICATION

If you and a partner have decided that you're ready to be sexually active, the next step should be talking to your partner about your sexual health and pregnancy prevention—and this exercise will help. Here are some examples of conversation-starters:

- Have you ever been tested for STIs before?
- So, we talked about sex but we haven't really talked about protection, pregnancy, or STIs ... what do you think about that?
- I'm nervous about STIs and I think we should get tested.
- We should probably talk about how we would handle it if I got pregnant.
- I'll feel a lot more comfortable if I know we're being safe.

Think of some other ways that you can start this conversation with a partner if you need to; maybe write them down in your journal if you feel it's useful.

Remember that in a safe and healthy relationship, your partner will be able to have this conversation with you, and they'll respect your boundaries and limits around sexual health and protection.

Of course, no method of protection is 100 percent guaranteed to be successful. So, it's worth knowing about what to do if you do get an STI, to make sure your choices when it comes to sex are truly informed and empowered.

## Coping with Getting an STI

The first thing to know here is that when people talk about health, sometimes sexual health gets stigmatized (negatively judged). But the reality is, everyone has a body, and all of our bodies can get sick—physically, mentally, or sexually. STIs are health issues—and no one should ever be made to feel ashamed of having a health issue! STIs are contracted from other people, like catching a flu, and they can be treated and managed.

Some STIs, like chlamydia or gonorrhea, are curable and they will go away after taking antibiotics or other treatment (Healthline 2018).

You can make sure that you know the symptoms, so you can recognize what has happened, and work from there to make sure you and your partners get tested, get treatment, and take precautions in the future. If you experience symptoms such as a rash, soreness, itching, burning, or anything else that doesn't feel normal for you, make sure to go to a doctor to get tested. Those symptoms don't necessarily mean that you have an STI (other common infections can cause similar symptoms), but you should still get tested to make sure you get the right treatment. Also, know that some STIs have no symptoms at all.

There are also other STIs—like HIV, herpes, HPV, and others—that are incurable. Some people may need medications or treatments to manage them. These STIs can have a lasting impact on a person; they can even be life-threatening (Healthline 2018). It's worth knowing about them if you're going to be sexually active, and we're here to help you navigate this. It's also important to keep in mind that it's wrong to stigmatize this or any health condition. Again, STIs are health issues, and no one should be made to feel shame for those.

Let's take a look at Billie experience below.

*A couple weeks ago, Billie got tested. The doctor called her and told her that she has an STI and that there's no cure for it. The doctor said that this STI isn't life-threatening and that there are treatments to manage it, but Billie will need to tell her previous partner and any future partners about it.*

*Billie's been feeling so upset about this. She feels dirty and disgusting, and like she can never date again, and she doesn't know what to do. Some nights she just sits in her room and cries. Her parents don't know what's wrong with her, and she can't even tell them. At school, her friend Suriaya saw her crying on the way to the counselor's office, and Billie ended up telling Suriaya what had happened—because she felt like her friend would be able to help support her.*

Billie is doing everything right. First of all, she got tested for STIs, which was a really mature and responsible thing to do. It also sounds like she has gone to talk to her counselor at school about this, which is great because they can help her through it. Finally, she opened up to her friend Suraiya, whom she feels she can trust.

It's a brave and mature gesture on Billie's part to begin understanding what's happened to her as part of her life that she should and *can* be open about, to the people she trusts. And the more support she can get, the better! She can continue to talk to her counselor, to help her with the feelings of low self-esteem she's been experiencing, so she can feel confident again, in life in general and in her relationships. If she wants, she can even join a support group, either in-person or online, so she can talk to other people who are in the same position she's in and can help her with what she's feeling and dealing with.

Having an STI can have a big impact on your life; it can potentially affect your health, self-esteem, reproductive ability, and more. However, it doesn't have to define who you are or your worth! People with STIs are able to live full and happy lives, date, get married, and have kids—it's all a matter of knowing your status and taking the necessary steps to protect and care for yourself and others. There can be a lot of stigma (judgment) surrounding sex and STIs, and many of us can feel really bad about ourselves if we get one. This is especially true considering the way society sometimes uses words like "clean" to describe when you are STI-free—the opposite of which is "dirty," which is an awful way to think of oneself. So, know this: if you ever contract an STI, it doesn't mean that you're "dirty." You are beautiful, lovable, and entirely capable of dating and having relationships. STIs are very common and you are not alone in this.

If you feel embarrassed or scared to tell your previous or future partners that you have an STI (whether it's curable or not), know that while it'll likely be really hard, you do have to take it seriously. It is important, on a legal *and* an ethical level, to be honest with your partners about your sexual history and their risk of infection.

Many people with STIs choose to wait until they feel comfortable with the person they are dating before sharing this information with them. That way, they can make a decision together about what they are okay with. That's totally okay, and it's often wise. Just remember: you *do* eventually have to tell the person you are with, before you get intimate with them. And you *can* do this in a way that respects your feelings and your partner's. Remember that any STI you or your partners have will *not* automatically define you or your relationship. And remember that while your partners have the right to make the decisions they feel comfortable with about whether or not they want to proceed with the relationship, if your partner loves and respects you, they won't judge you or make you feel bad for disclosing any part of your history to them.

Next, you'll find an exercise that will help you build yourself a support system, in case you ever need one to deal with a tough experience like the one Kat went through.

## EXERCISE: BUILDING YOUR SUPPORT SYSTEM

In the example above, Billie is relying on support from her friend Suriaya, as well as her school counselor, to help her cope with her diagnosis. Any time we go through a challenge in our lives, it's important to think about who we have in our corner who can help us, listen to us, or just cheer us up.

Take a minute or two to think about who you have in your life that is part of your support system. Then grab your journal and write them down! You might include your parents or guardians, other caregivers, friends, teachers or coaches, spiritual leaders in your community, your therapist or counselor, nurses, social workers, grandparents, aunts, uncles, cousins, romantic partners, etc.

If you don't feel like you have anyone who can support you, remember that there are many twenty-four-hour hotlines that you can call or text if you ever need someone to talk to. Many of these hotlines are listed in the Resources section at the back of the book.

## Let's Recap: Sexual Health

Talking about sexual health can sometimes be uncomfortable, but it doesn't have to be. Sexual health is just as important as the rest of our health! Let's recap what you've learned about STIs, pregnancy prevention, and sexual safety.

**Knowledge:** Ultimately, the key to making empowered decisions in your sex life is the same here as it is with anything. Make sure you're informed about sexually transmitted infections, the possibility of pregnancy, methods of contraception you might want to use, and your partners' romantic and sexual histories. It'll help you to make the best decisions possible for safe and healthy sex.

**Communication and Protection:** STIs and unplanned pregnancies can have a big impact on a person. Make sure you talk to your partner about both getting tested and pregnancy prevention, before you do anything physical. If you don't feel like you're ready to have this conversation, then you might not be ready to have sex. If you have an STI, make sure you communicate this to any past and future partners. Then, make sure you protect yourself, every time, no matter what type of sex you are having. If your partner doesn't want to use protection, then they might not respect you or your health. You can also protect yourself by getting tested regularly if you are sexually active.

**Treatment and Rights:** If you or your partner contract an STI, or need support with reproductive health resources, make sure that you seek treatment. Follow any recommendations you get from healthcare professionals carefully. And consider how you'll tell your partner, as you need to, either now or in the future. Check your state laws regarding your rights to access medical services for STI testing, pregnancy testing, and treatment. Many states provide minors the right to receive confidential STI/pregnancy testing and treatment and birth control methods, even during the school day. There's more information on this, if you need it, in the back of the book.

# CHAPTER 10

# Breakups Are Tough—but So Are You

As we've seen in the earlier chapters, dating and relationships can be really fun, and they can bring a lot of happiness. Other times we may need to end a relationship because it doesn't serve us anymore. Whether you broke up with your partner or they broke up with you, going through a breakup can be a super painful and difficult experience.

When you're with someone and things are good, it can make you feel incredibly special and happy. Some adults think that teen relationships aren't serious, but the reality is that the love that you feel for someone at sixteen can be just as intense as when you're forty! And it can be really upsetting to break up with someone and lose that feeling.

It's also important to remember that your relationships are just one part of your life. Who you are isn't defined by who you're dating; your self-worth doesn't depend on your relationship. People can break up for all kinds of reasons: timing, unhealthy dynamics, meeting someone else, different priorities, and more. And when you break up with someone, it doesn't necessarily mean that the relationship was a failure, or erase all that was good about your relationship. Often, even relationships that end badly or breakups that are difficult have something to teach us.

Sometimes a breakup is mutual, when both people realize it's not working for them anymore. Other times, one person is the one who decides to end the relationship. The decision whether or not to end a relationship can be a complicated one. When you think about your relationship, you want to ask yourself if it is still right for you. Is your relationship aligned with the values you identified in Chapter 1? Is it healthy? Or are there some unhealthy dynamics, like what you read about in Chapter 6?

Take your time making this decision if you need to. You don't have to figure out what to do in one day. If you do decide to break up with your partner, this chapter will give you the tools to be able to do that in a healthy and respectful way.

What if you're the one who got broken up with? If you're going through a breakup, remember that there's no magic formula for how long it takes to get over someone. It can be a big change to go from seeing someone every day, for instance, to not seeing them much at all—or to figure out how you'll spend the time you used to spend with them. But when you set good boundaries with yourself and with your ex (like taking a break from talking to them and following them on social media), it can make it easier to move forward. Sometimes, right after a breakup, it may feel like you'll never get over not seeing an ex as much as you did; or you might think you want to be friends with your ex in the future. But by the time you get over the relationship and move on to more exciting things in life, you might not even care if you talk to your ex or not!

In the end, breakups can be a learning experience; they teach us about ourselves, our strengths, and what we want out of a relationship. It is definitely possible to feel happy, special, and loved post-breakup! We're here to help you figure out how to cope with your breakup, how to set boundaries with your ex, how to find help getting over a breakup if you need it, and how to move on with your life—because you deserve to be happy.

## When Relationships End

Relationships can end for all kinds of reasons. Regardless of the reason, it's important to consider how you can handle a breakup in a mature and healthy way. During breakups, it's best if each person can communicate in a respectful way, and that each person can discuss what they want moving forward. Sometimes this is easier said than done, but in this chapter we'll help you to look at how you can navigate breakups in a way that can help you move forward in a healthy way.

Timing is an important factor in relationships, and sometimes things end because it isn't the right time. It can be really painful when two people love each other and they only break up because one person moves away, goes off to college, or has to focus on school. Let's look at Isa's experience: *Isa's boyfriend, Damon, is a senior, and she's a junior. He's graduating next month, and then he's going to college all the way in Pennsylvania, while Isa's staying in their home state for at least another year. They've been together for over a year and even though they talked about trying to stay together, Damon tells Isa he's not sure he can do a long-distance relationship. He suggests they break up after the school year is over.*

*Isa understands the decision—she's not sure she can do a long-distance relationship either—but it makes her so sad that she feels like crying every time she thinks about him leaving.*

Even though Isa and Damon both love each other, they've talked about what's realistic for their relationship and realize that they probably won't be able to keep dating. That's a difficult but mature conversation to have! They talked about their options, and even though breaking up will be really hard and sad, they care about each other, and Isa supports Damon's goals.

What can Isa do to help herself cope? For one thing, she could make the most of the next month by enjoying the time that she and Damon have left together. She could also make sure that she has a good support network ready to help her when they break up. She can spend time with friends, plan different fun activities, focus on school, and talk to her family/support system. If she gives herself things to look forward to and people to help her through it, it will be easier for her when they break up.

If you're in this situation, and you and your partner have to break up because of timing or different priorities, it's important to talk it through with your partner and come to an understanding. We're not saying that long distance is impossible or that you can't make difficult circumstances work (many relationships can overcome lots of obstacles!). We're just saying that sometimes life can get in the way and couples break up so that they can both pursue their own goals and priorities. Whatever you ultimately decide, we applaud you for knowing what's best for you!

Breaking up can be stressful and confusing at times. It's helpful to learn how to handle these difficult decisions, conversations, and feelings, so you'll feel more empowered to be able to handle these situations in a way that feels right for you. In the next section, we'll take a look at how to navigate the breakup conversation.

# Having the Conversation

Breaking up with someone can bring up a variety of feelings. For some who have chosen to end a relationship, it can feel liberating, freeing, and can give you a sense of peace to successfully end a relationship that isn't right for you anymore. For others, the idea of breaking up with someone can cause a sense of fear and dread over the thought of hurting someone and having a difficult conversation. Let's take a look at Hailey's experience when she broke up with her girlfriend, Kaliyah.

> Hailey and her girlfriend, Kaliyah, had been dating for a few months. At first, things had been going really well, but as time went on they started to have a lot of problems. They both had a tendency to get jealous, and then they would accuse each other of lying about something and it would turn into a big argument. Usually they would make up and things would be fine again for a while, but the same problems just kept coming up. They both knew it was a problem and they had tried to work on it, but things just weren't getting better.
>
> So, Hailey decided to end the relationship. She knew she probably should have broken up with Kaliyah in person, but she got so mad one day during an argument they were having over text that she just ended it then and there,

*by text. Now Kaliyah is devastated and Hailey feels bad for how she ended it and the things she said during the argument.*

Sometimes breakups can be messy, like when people break up during the middle of a heated argument and say hurtful things. In this situation, even though Hailey cared about Kaliyah, she recognized that this relationship dynamic wasn't healthy for her. Unfortunately, she broke up with Kaliyah angrily over text instead of being able to talk to her in person, like she'd planned to. In this section, we'll take a look at ways that you can respectfully break up with your partner, which will make it easier on both of you in the long run.

How, when, where, and why should you have the breakup conversation? Once you've decided to end your relationship for whatever reason, it's best to consider your next steps carefully. Ideally, you'll have the conversation with your partner in person, in a private place (if it's safe to do so), when you both have some time to talk things through as calmly and respectfully as you can. If you can, it's best to avoid situations like Hailey's, where both people are angry, saying hurtful things, and texting rather than talking.

You might be thinking, "Okay but what do I actually say? I don't want to hurt my partner's feelings!" Before having the conversation, think about what you'd like to say. You might want to reflect on your values and priorities, and what's not working in the relationship. You'll want to be honest and direct with your partner, but also sensitive to their feelings.

Let's take a look at the exercise below, to practice.

# EXERCISE: BREAKUP CONVERSATION

When you end a relationship with someone, it can be hard to know what to say or how to say it. Find a time when both of you are able to talk, and speak in a calm and respectful tone if you can. Here are some examples of some breakup conversation-starters:

1. I need to talk with you about something. Lately I've been feeling _____ and I don't think this relationship is working for me anymore.
2. I really care about you and I don't want to hurt your feelings. But you should know that I _____. Because of this, I don't think we can keep dating.
3. I know this is hard to hear, but I think we should break up.
4. I want to be honest with you. I think we both deserve that. So I need to tell you that I've been feeling _____.
5. There are a lot of good things about our relationship, like _____. But there are other things that just aren't working for me, like

_____. I just don't think we should keep seeing each other.

Write your own! We know that these conversations aren't easy to have. But if you carefully consider what you need to say to your partner, and how to do it respectfully, it will make it easier for everyone involved.

But what if you're on the receiving end of the breakup, like Kaliyah? How is she supposed to respond when Hailey breaks up with her by text? Kaliyah was already feeling really angry during the argument, and now she's feeling devastated that Hailey broke up with her so suddenly. If you've been broken up with, especially if it was in a sudden or hurtful way, it's important to think carefully about how to respond.

It's normal during a breakup to become upset, cry, get angry, or want to say hurtful things. These can be really strong and valid feelings! But remember that your partner is someone who you care about. Even if the relationship is ending, this is still someone you cared for and they deserve respect and honesty. You are certainly allowed to express your feelings during a breakup conversation, but try to avoid name-calling, yelling, or hurtful statements. If you can express your feelings respectfully, this will be a healthier and more productive conversation for everyone. Here are some examples of what this might look like:

1. I can't believe this is happening. Are you sure? I'm really caught off guard by this.
2. Is this really what you want? Can you explain to me why?
3. I'm really _____ right now. I need to take some time before I can talk to you.
4. Thank you for being honest with me about how you're feeling. Even though this is hard for me to hear, I'm glad you told me.
5. I can't imagine not talking to you all the time. Do you still want to be friends? Or do you think it's better if we don't talk for a while?

These are just a few examples. We know that these conversations can be really painful and hard and that no one is a perfect communicator—but speaking respectfully will make the process easier. You've got this!

As for Hailey and Kaliyah, this experience is one that they can learn from. Hailey understands that the breakup conversation didn't go well because she didn't talk to Kaliyah calmly, and in person, like she planned to. She could apologize to Kaliyah for the way she handled that conversation, and if she has to break up with someone again in the future, she can try to do things differently.

In the next section, we'll look at how to cope with some of the intense feelings that can arise during a breakup.

## Using Coping Skills to Deal with Strong Feelings

After a breakup, you might be experiencing really difficult feelings. A lot of us get caught up in our thoughts about the past—thinking nonstop, over and over again, about what happened and all the things that we regret. It can be hard to take our minds off how badly it hurts to be without the person we lost. Or we might end up worrying about the future: *Will I ever find someone who makes me feel the way my partner did?*

These are situations in which it can be useful to have some activities you can do to cope with what you feel—to make yourself feel cared for and practice self-compassion. It can be very hard to be without your partner, especially if the relationship lasted a long time. It's normal to really miss your ex. But you can learn how to take care of yourself when you're in pain, by figuring out what you can do to de-stress and cheer up, or at least take your mind off what you're going through for a little while.

Take a look at the exercise below to help you learn how to cope with the difficult feelings you might be having during a breakup.

# EXERCISE: USING HEALTHY COPING SKILLS

Coping skills help you to get through difficult times by allowing you to feel better, relax, de-stress, and distract from your current situation. Here are some examples of coping skills:

Exercising
Talking to Friends
Spending Time with Family
Walking Your Dog
Listening to Music
Journaling
Crafting
Deep Breathing
Meditating
Stretching
Cooking
Watching a Funny Movie
Baking
Spiritual Practice
Playing an Instrument
Spending Time in Nature
Singing
Taking a Bath
Reading

Now write your own! Grab your journal and make a list of your favorite things to do that can help you to de-stress or cheer up.

It's worth knowing that sometimes, especially when we're going through something tough, we might try to cope in unhealthy ways that end up making us feel worse in the long run. Let's take a look at the chart below for some do's and don'ts—some examples of unhelpful coping, or ways of coping that may make you feel worse, not better, paired with a healthier alternative that has a better chance of actually helping you.

| Unhelpful Coping Skill | Helpful Coping Skill Alternative |
|---|---|
| Spend all day in bed crying | Cry for a little while and then take a walk outside |
| Spend hours looking at pics of your ex | Make a craft collage of pics of your friends |
| Obsess over your ex's social media—where they are and who they're with | Turn off your phone and read a book |
| Show up at your ex's house unannounced | Stay home and watch a funny movie with a friend or sibling |
| Post negative messages on your social media for others to see and react to | Journal about your feelings, to really see them and sort them out |
| Hurt yourself in some way | Schedule a therapy session or call a hotline |
| Sit in the dark all day long in your PJs | Take a refreshing shower and walk the dog/exercise |

| | |
|---|---|
| Talk badly about your ex to everyone you know | Make a list of your strengths and good qualities so you can keep them in mind |
| Numb the pain with drugs or alcohol | Call or spend time with a friend |
| Blow up your ex's phone with messages/calls | Give your ex space so each of you can process your own feelings |

You'll see that a lot of the positive coping skills above involve setting good boundaries between yourself and your ex. If you are going through a breakup, it's really important to set boundaries so that you can move on—to be clear with one another about what you need to heal.

## Setting Boundaries after a Breakup

Some couples can stay friends after breaking up, but sometimes that's too difficult because it can make the process of getting over the person harder. When you keep talking to each other, it's hard to let go of the feelings you have for the person. Especially if they start dating someone new, it can be really painful to have to see and hear about their new relationship. If you set boundaries with your ex, it will be easier to move on.

When it comes to social media, it gets even more complicated. Social media can make breakups pretty tough, since on a lot of platforms you can basically see what your ex is doing, where they are, and who they're with any time you want. This can make it really difficult to move on. It can also make it hard not to compare yourself to other people, especially people who might be in happy relationships of their own, which can make you feel worse about your situation. It's sort of like when you drive past a car accident and can't look away—painful to look at, and probably not the best idea!

Let's look at how Lucy felt when her ex-boyfriend Vince started dating someone new.

> *Lucy and her boyfriend Vince just broke up after being together for two months. He said he needed to break up because he had to focus on school since he's failing some classes, but he's already posting pics on social media with a new girl. Even though she and Vince only dated for a couple months, Lucy really liked him. They agreed to stay friends, so sometimes Lucy messages Vince just to say hi, but he seems like he doesn't care anymore. To make matters worse, Lucy's friend Daya keeps telling her what Vince is doing, even on the days Lucy decides she won't check on what he's doing online. She doesn't know how she can get over this and stop feeling bad all the time, especially with Daya being involved.*

This is painful! Lucy and Vince were dating for a couple months, and even though it was a short time, it felt serious. Now Lucy's trying to find a way to get over her ex. It might be difficult, but Lucy could unfollow Vince on social media so that she can't see his posts anymore. She could also be clear with him that even though she might like to be friends with him in the future, she needs some space from him and won't be contacting him right now. She could also be honest with her friend Daya and tell her that she'd rather not hear about who Vince is dating; it's just making it harder for her to move on. Lucy can also try to distract herself and practice self-care: making plans with friends, exercising, listening to music, making art, and journaling. When she fills up her days with healthy outlets and things that she enjoys doing, it will make it easier for her to keep her boundaries and eventually move on.

Remember, it is OKAY to feel sad after a breakup and it can take time to get over someone. Sometimes you may need to give yourself time to cry it out (maybe while listening to a breakup playlist). But after you let yourself feel sad, make sure you take care of yourself. Do things that you enjoy that fill you up, and spend time talking to your friends or loved ones—you don't have to go through it alone. It will get easier, we promise.

Let's take a look at the exercise below to learn about setting boundaries.

## EXERCISE: SETTING BOUNDARIES

Boundaries are the limits we set for ourselves with other people or situations. During a breakup, it can be helpful to let your ex know what you're comfortable with when it comes to communication and social media. This is different for everyone and only you know what will feel right for you. Here are some examples of how you can communicate healthy boundaries with your ex after you've broken up:

1. I know we still have classes together, but it's hard for me to keep seeing you at lunch with our friends. I think it would be better if I ate lunch with a different group of people for a while.
2. I still care about you, but I can't keep talking to you every day. It's making it harder for me to move on.
3. I might want to be friends with you again in the future, but for now I have to unfollow you on social media so that I can focus on myself.
4. I don't want to hurt your feelings, but I need to block you for a while so that I can feel better.
5. I'm okay with _____ but I'd rather not _____.

Write your own! Only you know what boundaries you're comfortable setting with your ex. Grab a piece of paper and write down what you could say to an ex if you were trying to set boundaries about communication.

## When You're Worried About Your Partner After a Breakup

Going through a breakup can be a painful experience for everyone involved. Ideally, we'll be able to rely on the support of our friends and family to help us cope with the breakup and have healthy boundaries with an ex. But sometimes breakups, like all painful experiences, can affect a person's physical or mental health. And you might find yourself in a position where you're concerned about your ex's health, in addition to your own. Let's look at Charlotte's experience, when she became worried about her ex-boyfriend Beau after they broke up.

*Charlotte broke up with her boyfriend, Beau, because she found out that he cheated on her. But ever since they broke up, he's been messaging her nonstop, saying how sorry he is and that he can't live without her. She can't tell if he's serious or not. She doesn't want to get back together with him and she's so mad at him for cheating on her, but from the tone of his messages she's wondering if he might be seriously depressed or even suicidal. She's not sure what to do.*

Charlotte is doing a few things right here. First of all, she's standing up for herself and what she needs in a relationship. She knows that it's not okay that her boyfriend cheated on her, and she knows that she deserves a healthy relationship where she can trust the person she's with. She's not giving in to the pressure to get back together with him, even though she misses him sometimes.

As for Beau, it seems he's feeling pretty guilty about what he did. In his messages to Charlotte, he's been telling her that he needs her back in his life and that he "can't live without her." Although this is vague, it's part of a pattern of depressed and hopeless behavior. Charlotte doesn't know if Beau's safe or not—and while she's upset at him for cheating on her, she doesn't want him to hurt himself or be unsafe either.

It's really important to take something like this seriously, even if you're not completely sure what's going on with someone's mental health. Some people think teens express suicidal thoughts "to get attention." That's usually not the case. But even if the person isn't ultimately at active risk of harming themselves, it's better to be safe than sorry; it's a good thing to care about others' well-being, even if it's someone who's hurt you in the past. If Beau is serious, then it's important that he gets the help he needs.

Charlotte should let him know that she's worried about him and encourage him to get help—while still keeping the boundaries she's set (like the fact that she doesn't want to get back together with him). She should also talk to a trusted adult, to let them know what's going on so that they can help Beau get help if he needs it.

If you're in a situation like this, and you're worried that your ex is depressed and potentially unsafe because of the breakup, it doesn't mean you have to stay with them. Whether as someone's partner or as their ex, you're not responsible for taking care of anyone else's mental health. Your only job is to let an adult know what's going on, so that your ex can get the help they need to stay safe.

## Coming to Terms with a Breakup

What if you're feeling depressed after a breakup—in a way that coping skills and self-care can only go so far to fix? This can happen and your feelings are valid. And you don't have to go through it alone. Make sure you get help and reach out for support. Know that even if it doesn't feel like it right now, the pain you feel will get easier to deal with in time (we promise!), and you will feel better in the future.

There are also skills you can use to give yourself some comfort and peace about what happened to you, even as you acknowledge how painful it is for your relationship to be over. Let's take a look at the exercise below to help turn your breakup into a helpful learning experience.

## EXERCISE: REFRAMING YOUR THOUGHTS

In a breakup, you may not be able to change the situation, but you *can* change the way you think about it. Cognitive reframing is a technique that you can use to change the way that you think about something. It's about taking the thoughts that are negative or not-so-helpful, seeing if they're really accurate or useful thoughts to have, and figuring out new thoughts that might better help you cope with what you feel. With cognitive restructuring, you can take your negative thoughts and turn them into more-helpful ones—ones that see the breakup as a learning experience or even as an opportunity. Take a look at the examples below:

| Negative Thought | Helpful Alternative |
| --- | --- |
| I'll never find anyone else. | There are a lot of great people out there for me to meet. |
| I'm going to be alone forever. | There's nothing wrong with being single! I get time for me. |
| No one loves me. | I have family and friends who love me. |
| My ex treated me so badly. | I learned a lot about how I want and deserve to be treated. |
| I should never have dated him. | I know a lot now about what I want in my next relationship. |

| | |
|---|---|
| I wish they would call me. | I have so much time to focus on school, friends, and family. |
| I don't have anyone to hang out with after school. | My grades are getting better now. |
| Was I not good enough for him? | I know I have a lot to offer. I'm a really caring person. |
| What does she have that I don't? | Everyone has great qualities. My friends say I'm really funny. |
| I'll never trust anyone again. | I'm learning how to tell when a relationship is unhealthy |

Write your own! Are you having negative thoughts about a breakup? Write down your negative thoughts in your journal and then challenge yourself to turn them into helpful ones.

Breakups can sometimes be really hard on your self-esteem and how you feel about yourself. It's important to remember all of your good qualities and what makes you unique! If you're having trouble thinking of some positive qualities, try to think about what your closest friends and family would say about you. For example, they might say that you are kind, trustworthy, loyal, funny.... You can also flip back to the "Less Comparing, More Strength-Finding" exercise in Chapter 2, to be reminded of the many parts of you that you like and are proud of. In the end, when we can shift our perspective about what's happened to us from an unhelpful one to a more-helpful one, and keep our own positive qualities in mind as we try to move on, it makes breakups and any other painful experiences a lot easier to cope with.

Know that it's also okay to ask for more help if you need it. Talk to friends, family, and other trusted adults in your life about how you feel. Get help, like therapy, if you feel you need it. And check the resources in the back of the book for more help with all of this. Never forget that you are strong, worthy, and beautiful—inside and out!

## Let's Recap: Breakups

Going through a breakup can be a difficult experience, regardless of who broke up with whom or why. But we know you can get through it! Come back to this recap anytime you need some help going through a split with a partner.

**Boundaries:** Getting over a breakup is easier if you set healthy boundaries (limits) with your ex—if you're not constantly seeing them, in touch, or keeping tabs on them. You could try taking a break from talking to each other and unfollowing them on social media.

**Coping:** It can be really tough to cope with a breakup. Make sure you have a good support network of friends, family, and/or a counselor/therapist, and that you are using your healthy coping skills and habits that'll help you take care of yourself. If you're trying everything but still feeling depressed, always know you can reach out to a professional for more help. If you're worried about your ex's safety after a breakup, make sure to ask for help. After a breakup, try to remind yourself of your great qualities and what makes you YOU! Your fundamental self-worth is not defined by your relationship. You're enough, just as you are, and you always will be.

**Safety and Mental Health:** Breakups can take a toll on your mental health or that of your ex. If you or an ex are experiencing depressive thoughts or thoughts of self-harm, seek help. You are not alone.

# CHAPTER 11

# Some News About Sexting and Nudes

A big part of dating today involves texting and social media. Phones have become a way to flirt, express feelings, or show someone that you're thinking about them. While communicating this way is common and convenient, it also comes with some challenges and uncomfortable situations. Regardless of where you are in your dating and relationship journey, it's important for you to think about and clarify your limits when it comes to the use of technology. In this chapter, you'll read about common situations, become familiar with some of the legal issues that can come up if you're exchanging explicit images or content, and learn some skills so you can feel more confident confronting these pressures.

## Knowing and Expressing What You're Comfortable With

In the early stages of a relationship, you are getting to know your partner and your partner is getting to know you. While the "honeymoon" stage can be exciting, there can also be some anxiety about messing it up, or feelings of insecurity. Sometimes you might try to impress your partner or prove how much you care. Other times you might try to avoid conversations or situations that you think could cause a fight or breakup. The scenario below between Shakira and her partner offers an example of a newer relationship and how it can be difficult to express feelings and set limits with a partner.

> *Shakira has been dating her partner, Dev, for two months. She thinks it's going well, and her feelings are starting to grow. She met Dev's parents and Dev met her family. Shakira has fun with Dev and they get along with each other's friends.*
>
> *Recently, Dev asked Shakira to send her "sexy" pics. Shakira's not sure she wants to send the pics; she trusts Dev, but she's not sure she trusts the technology. Of course, she doesn't want Dev to think she doesn't love them either.*

It can be really hard to say "no" when your partner or someone you are talking to asks for pics. Even if you trust them completely or have been together for years, you still might not feel comfortable or okay with it—either because it feels weird to take the pictures, or because you, like Shakira, aren't really sure you trust that anyone can keep them private or safeguard against the possibility that they might be leaked.

In the end, it's your face and body, so whether to take a photo or not is always your call. Even if you are dating someone who you love or care about, you don't owe them anything. Sometimes your partner may push, but as you know by now, if they don't respect your limits, this is a problem; in a healthy relationship, your partner will respect and honor your feelings and boundaries.

In Shakira's case, she should be firm and communicate this boundary she has to her partner, saying something like, "Dev, I love you, but I don't think I want to send you any sexy pics. I'm not comfortable having photos of myself out there like that. It's not that I don't trust you; I'm just not comfortable doing this." If Dev is understanding and respects this boundary, that's awesome. Sometimes these conversations can help a relationship, by clarifying what each person is and is not okay with. If Dev continues to push Shakira or pressure her to do anything she is not okay with, Shakira should reevaluate the relationship. She should be in a relationship that feels safe—one that allows her to assert herself and set limits.

What if you find yourself in a similar situation? While it may not always be easy, we support you in asserting yourself. Maybe say, "No, I'm not sending you that" or "No, I'm not comfortable with that." You don't have to overexplain or justify why. If your partner makes a big deal about it—well, you'll know that this may not be someone who respects your boundaries or someone you can feel safe with.

It's always important to check in with yourself, to remind yourself of what's important to you and what you need to feel safe in a relationship, and to make the decisions that feel best for you. Partners and others in your life might push and test your boundaries, and you might have to stand up for yourself, and even end relationships. But when you set limits and honor your values and beliefs, you'll feel empowered and good about yourself in the long-term, even if in the short-term it leads to some uncomfortable conversations.

In this next exercise, take some time to self-reflect and figure out what kinds of limits you might want to set for yourself and your partners when it comes to texting.

## EXERCISE: SETTING LIMITS WITH TECHNOLOGY

Sometimes you might be certain of your limits and know exactly what you are okay or not okay with. Other times you might have no clue, or just haven't given it much thought. Your limits can also change over the course of a relationship.

Knowing your limits ahead of time can be helpful, because you can communicate them in your relationships with more confidence. Take a moment to think about your limits and the things you need to feel safe in a relationship—both physically and emotionally. Grab your journal or a piece of paper and write them down.

*Examples:*

> I'm not okay with my boyfriend sending me dick pics.
> I'm not okay with sending nudes.
> I don't want to have sex until I'm older.
> I'm okay with having my partner over if someone in my family is home.

We encourage you to revisit these limits in the future, especially if you are having a difficult time navigating uncomfortable situations or having to communicate them to your partner or someone you're dating.

## Why Having Boundaries and Being Careful Matters

Relationships can be passionate and exciting, which can make it easy to get caught up in the moment. And when we are in a relationship with someone we really care about, we often want to please them. While sending a flirty text or picture might not seem like a big deal, we want you to have all the information to make informed decisions when it comes to what you text or share with a partner. The scenario below provides an example of how sending an explicit picture could have more lasting effects.

> *Diamond sent her ex-boyfriend Josue very personal pictures of her when they were still together. She took and sent those pictures just for him. They broke up two weeks ago and now her friend Sammi tells Diamond the pictures were leaked to his friends. Diamond's really worried and doesn't know what to do.*

This is why sending nudes or explicit pictures to others can be risky. It's clear that the photos Diamond took for Josue were personal and meant for him and him only, but now they have been shared with his friends, probably by Josue himself.

It may seem unimaginable that someone would do this. But breakups can be intense—and exes and even people you really loved can sometimes act in ways that you could never have imagined. This sort of thing can even happen while you're still in a relationship. What's important to know is that sharing explicit pictures of minors can have both legal and long-term consequences, as you'll see below. This makes it especially important for you to think carefully about the boundaries we talked about in the last section.

If something like what happened to Diamond happens to you, here are some things you can take into consideration—and some options for what you want to do next.

**Internet circulation:** With technology these days, a picture or text can be easily found by unintended viewers (friends, classmates, or even strangers online) or sent without you even being aware. Those pictures that may have been intended for a specific person could end up in the depths of the Internet. While we would like to believe that when we "delete" a picture or text it's gone forever, nothing that's posted online is ever truly gone; there's always a chance that it could resurface. Think about it this way—in a few years from now, when you're applying for a job or school, there is always a possibility that something you posted to social media or sent to another person could pop up in a Google search.

**The importance of age:** If you're under eighteen, by law you're still a child—and nudes or other similarly explicit material of minors may be classified as child porn. This means that even if there was mutual consent when a picture was sent or text messages were exchanged, if sexual content involving a minor were to surface, both the person receiving the text and the person sending it could face legal consequences—which can vary by country and state.

So, what are Diamond's options? First, Diamond should ask for support and guidance from a trusted adult. This might be uncomfortable and hard to do. But if she doesn't address this, the pictures could continue to get passed around, making it even more difficult to stop or intervene. Diamond should also know that what her ex did is against the law, and she has the right to hold her ex and those who are involved accountable if she wants to. Talking to an adult she trusts can also help Diamond decide what options for legal action she or her family might want to explore. Finally, Diamond should consider if she needs help dealing with the psychological and emotional stress of going through something like this, which is profoundly unfair and can be extremely stressful. Talking to trusted adults about how she feels can help make this very tough thing she's dealing with at least a little easier.

What can you do if your own pictures have been leaked? While it may seem easier to ignore this completely, it is important to remember that you have rights in this situation. Many teen girls have found themselves in this situation and it can bring up feelings of shame, anger, guilt, anxiety, overwhelm, or all the above. Talking it out and having a safe space to process something like this can be incredibly helpful, and there are many people and resources available to you if you ever end up in this position. You can seek support from a school counselor or therapist, and check out the resources in the back of the book if you need more support.

You can also try to practice self-compassion, especially if you're feeling guilt or shame after an incident like the one that Diamond went through. These are understandable emotions to feel in such situations—but things like this, which are violations of your boundaries and your rights, are absolutely not your fault.

Let's break down and have you practice the skill of self-compassion.

## EXERCISE: PRACTICING SELF-COMPASSION

Having self-compassion means treating yourself with kindness and understanding. Instead of criticizing or shaming yourself for past decisions, or someone taking advantage of your trust and love, try validating your own feelings and giving yourself the same love and patience that you would give to a close friend. Shame doesn't help you to heal from something that's happened; in fact, it prolongs the pain you feel and makes it worse. Self-compassion can help you cope with uncomfortable feelings and work through difficult situations you might face in a healthy way.

Think of a time when you made a mistake or did something that you regretted. If it was your best friend coming to you with this problem, what would you tell them? You probably wouldn't shame them or be judgmental, would you? Instead, you might say something like, "I know this sucks, but we all make mistakes," or "I'd be upset too, but you are human and you'll be able to learn from this," or "What happened to you wasn't your fault. You'll learn from it and you'll heal."

Now take a moment and write down your own caring words that you would give a friend if they were going through the same thing you're going through. Keep these words and use them when you need reassurance and validation in the future. You can be as kind to yourself as you'd be to a friend; you deserve it.

## Navigating Unsolicited Pictures and Text Messages

A lot of teens prefer texting and messaging as their primary mode of communication, because of its convenience. When you're texting someone you're dating, it can be a lot easier to be vulnerable and say the things you want to say, versus if you were talking to them in person or even over the phone. As a result, teens (and adults) tend to feel more comfortable and confident over text. Even with these benefits, there can also be unwanted contact and communication when texting or messaging.

Take a look at the situation below, which provides an example of what this might look like.

*Jolie was messaging a guy, Sam, that she met through one of her best guy friends. Over the last couple weeks, they've been messaging pretty much nonstop. She liked Sam, and thought he was cute and funny—but last night he sent her a dick pic without warning. Jolie didn't ask for the pic and feels uncomfortable about it. But she doesn't want Sam to stop liking or talking to her either.*

Sam's done a few things wrong here. First, he sent an explicit picture to Jolie—who's fifteen years old—and that's considered illegal. This picture was also unsolicited, meaning that Jolie did not ask for it or consent to receive it. Explicit texts and pictures like this need consent; it's no different than with sexual activity. You might sometimes feel like you have to be "nice" or "understanding" in a moment like this—especially if it's with someone you know or like—but the fact is, you don't have to tolerate anything that you're not okay or comfortable with.

So what should Jolie do? First, she should be clear with Sam that what he did was wrong—a violation of her boundaries. She should be clear and direct with Sam that she didn't ask for this photo and that she doesn't want him to send her photos like this again.

Of course, Jolie doesn't have to say anything to Sam at all. She could also simply not respond, end the conversation, or block him on social media completely—whatever she needs to do in order to feel safe. Even if it might feel awkward or uncomfortable, she can also let a parent or trusted adult know what happened, so they can help her figure out her options and help keep her safe going forward.

What should you do if you're in a situation like this? Bottom line: If you ever feel uncomfortable or question the intentions of someone you're with or just talking to, go with your gut. If what's happening feels uncomfortable to you, that in and of itself is a sign that you have a boundary that the other person is violating. Honor your boundaries and your right to decide what happens to you! The right person will not make you feel pressured or uncomfortable. Know that you *can* take action and assert yourself through confronting, blocking, and reporting something like this.

Throughout this whole book, you've been working on your skills of self-reflection—checking in with yourself and what you feel and need, to figure out what you really want to do in any given situation—and assertive communication: learning how to speak up for what you need and deserve, and how to resist the pressure that people who don't have your best interests at heart may put on you.

When it comes to continuing to build your confidence to speak up for yourself, an exercise like the one that follows will help.

## EXERCISE: TAPPING INTO CONFIDENCE

In sensitive situations, standing up for yourself and confronting people can be difficult, especially if you struggle with confidence and self-esteem; it can make you doubt yourself—your judgment, your self-worth, or your ability to have and set standards for people you're dating. When you feel confident—when you develop the ability to know what's true for you, be certain about it, and express it to others without fear—it gets easier to assert yourself, speak up, and hold other people accountable.

Think about a person you admire or look up to that exudes confidence—this can be someone close to you or a public figure. As one example, you could imagine the Olympic gymnast Simone Biles up on a podium, answering questions about herself. She stands up straight, makes eye contact with reporters, and speaks firmly and steadily.

Now try it yourself. First, think of your confident person, and then ask yourself these questions:

What are some of the traits and qualities you like about this person?

Which of these traits and qualities do you share with this person? Or which qualities do you wish you could embody?

How might this person respond to a situation in which they are being disrespected?

Now visualize yourself as this confident person and ask yourself the following, picturing it in your head and noticing all the details:

What would you say to someone who disrespected you or crossed a boundary?

What would your body language be like?

What would your tone of voice be like?

Would anybody else be part of this conversation to help you?

Come back to and use this image in the future, when you need to tap into your confidence and assert yourself!

## Let's Recap: Sexting and Nudes

The knowledge you have gained in this chapter builds on what you have learned from the chapters you've read so far. You have the same rights on social media or on your phone that you have anywhere: to be treated with respect, to have others respect your boundaries, and to be loved and treated kindly by the people you come into contact with and enter relationships with. Let's recap what you learned about in this chapter:

**You Have Rights:** You have the right to be treated with respect and kindness. You have the right to say "no." You have the right to report and block anyone who violates these rights, and to assert yourself in order to feel safe. As a minor, you have laws that protect you from harmful sexual encounters, which are useful to know about. And know that you can always seek support or help from your parent or trusted adult if you find yourself in an unsafe or uncomfortable situation.

**You Don't Have to Prove Yourself:** Other people may sometimes behave as though it's normal to send sexts, nudes, and more, and like it's uncool not to. That's on them. You don't have to send pictures, receive pictures, or do anything that makes you feel unsafe or uneasy. You will still be just as worthy even if you don't send a pic or sext or engage in any online activity that makes you uncomfortable. And it's a sign of your self-knowledge and self-respect when you successfully understand and enforce your own boundaries. That's never a problem.

**Self-Compassion:** Shame isn't helpful to the healing process. Self-compassion can help you cope with uncomfortable feelings. If you've made decisions in the past that you could have handled differently, avoid self-criticism and try giving yourself the same love and patience that you would give to a close friend.

## PARTING GIFT

# Your Decisions Are the Power in Sexual Empowerment

You've made it to the end of this book! We've covered a lot in these chapters, and hopefully you've gained information that's useful and helpful, and gives you the confidence to feel and be empowered as you continue to grow and change.

Before we part ways, we want you to consider all of your strengths and some of the things you have learned! Take some time to reflect on these questions below:

- What are some of the things you have discovered about yourself in terms of your values, identity, self-worth, and body image?
- What are some of your strengths, and qualities that you like about yourself? Are there areas for growth or things you would like to work on? If so, how will you work on them?
- How do you feel about your friendships and relationships?

- What are some of the things that you value in a relationship and want in a partner?
- Do you know the difference between a healthy and an unhealthy relationship?
- What have you learned about your sexual health and communicating your needs in that department?

As you continue on your journey, there may be ups and downs. Some days you will feel confident and completely in charge! On the harder days, it is important to remember that nobody is perfect—that's part of being human. And you can learn and grow from each and every one of your experiences. We all do.

Now you have the tools you need to work through the things that come with being a young adult. You know more about yourself—what's important to you, the different parts of your identity, and the things you have learned to like and love about yourself. You know how to stand up for yourself and make decisions that feel right for *you*. And you know your rights! You have the right to be in a healthy relationship and to be treated with kindness and respect. You have the right to say "no" and to set limits and boundaries. But most important, you have the ability to make informed and empowered choices, based on your own personal values, that will support your physical and mental health!

In the years to come, you might make mistakes or mess up here and there; you might not always be able to make exactly the right decisions at exactly the right times. Know that this is a normal part of life as a teen and young adult, and it's okay—as long as you continue to check in with yourself, reflect on your actions and what's happening, and are willing to take responsibility when you need to, you'll be able to handle whatever comes, even when it's tough.

And remember, it's okay to ask for help! You can come back to this book as often as you need, but don't forget about your trusted adults and support system. It is *always* okay to lean on others and seek out support and guidance when you need it. You got this!

# Acknowledgments

We would like to take a moment to thank those who have been influential and impactful in the process of bringing this book to life.

To New Harbinger Publications, thank you for taking on this project and believing in the mission of this book—to empower young women in a way that has not been done before. Thank you to our editors, Georgia Kolias, Jennifer Holder, Vicraj Gill, and Teja Watson, for your enthusiasm, guidance, and hard work to make this book happen.

To Lisa Schab, thank you for inspiring us and connecting us to New Harbinger Publications, and for your thoughtfulness and time.

To our clients over the years, thank you for sharing your experiences with us. It has been an honor to work with you and we so appreciate you.

To our families and loved ones who have supported and encouraged us in this endeavor, thank you. To our parents who work in the mental health fields of social work and psychiatry, you have created a foundation and an admirable example for us to follow.

To our friends, thank you for the ongoing support and encouragement with this project. And to Pooja Nair for her invaluable support during the initial planning stage.

To our clinical supervisors, coworkers, and peers, thank you for providing a positive working environment and collaborative effort. Our consultations and collaboration have strengthened our skills and we appreciate you.

To the people who have read and reviewed our work, thank you for your time, feedback, and support. We know your time is valuable and are so grateful for your help.

# Resources

This section is designed to give you more detailed information on some of the topics we covered in this book! There's a ton of info out there and sometimes it can be hard to know what is accurate. That's why we've included some of the most up-to-date info available to help you figure things out and get the support you may need.

## Resources for Developing Values

Developing your values, in terms of your relationships and in general, is part of growing up. And knowing your values can help you feel more confident in making decisions. Here's a helpful link with a list of values for you to consider:

https://motivationalinterviewing.org/sites/default/files/valuescardsort_0.pdf

## Resources for LGBTQIA+ Youth

Understanding your sexual identity can sometimes be confusing or complicated. If you or someone you know is seeking support for questions about sexual identity, the resources below can help.

## Hotlines:

The Trevor Project Hotline: call (866) 488-7386, text 678678, or chat at https://www.thetrevorproject.org/get-help-now/

## Helpful websites:

https://www.thetrevorproject.org/resources/trevor-support-center/
https://itgetsbetter.org/
https://pflag.org/

# Resources for Navigating Unhealthy Relationships

If you or a friend are in a relationship that you think might be unhealthy, the resources below can help you out. Don't be afraid to ask questions or seek help if you need to. You can use the Power and Control Wheel as well as the Equality Wheel in this section to help you understand examples of unhealthy and healthy relationship behaviors.

## Hotlines:

National Domestic Violence Hotline: (800) 799-7233, (800) 787-3224 (TTY)
Love is Respect Hotline: (866) 331-9474; text LOVEIS to 22522

National Human Trafficking Hotline: (888) 373-7888

## Helpful Websites:

https://www.loveisrespect.org/

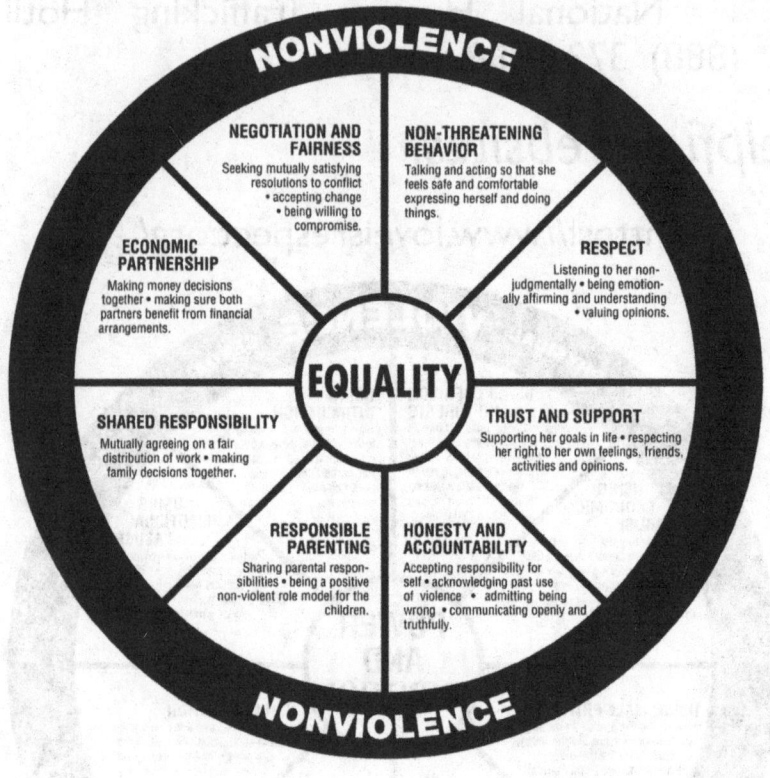

# Resources for Online Relationship Safety

Again, online relationships are real relationships too—and you should remember to always stay safe! Check out the following tips for online dating and relationships.

## Hotlines:

Crime Stoppers: (713) 222-8477

## Helpful Websites:

https://kidshelpline.com.au/teens/issues/staying-safe-online

https://www.connectsafely.org/social-web-tips-for-teens/

https://teens.webmd.com/features/teen-internet-safety-tips#1

# Resources for Breakups and Mental Health

Breakups can be really hard and can sometimes take a toll on your mental health. If you or someone you know is experiencing a mental health issue, you can seek help from the following resources. Don't be afraid to get the help that you need; your mental health and the mental health of people you know is valuable, and worth taking care of.

## Hotlines:

National Suicide Prevention Hotline: (800) 273-8255

Online Suicide Prevention Chat: https://suicidepreventionlifeline.org/chat/

Crisis Text Line: text 741741

Love Is Respect Hotline: (866) 331-9474

## *Helpful Websites:*

https://suicidepreventionlifeline.org/help-yourself/youth/
https://youmatter.suicidepreventionlifeline.org/?_ga=2.184617001.124917781.1578354188-1997104306.1578354188
https://www.activeminds.org/
https://www.thetrevorproject.org/
https://www.loveisrespect.org/
https://kidshealth.org/en/teens/broken-heart.html

# Resources for Sexual Assault

If you or someone you know has experienced unwanted sexual contact, call 911 or one of the hotlines below for immediate assistance. Additionally, the following information can help you. And remember: You are not alone! There are people and resources around to help you. Get yourself the help you need; you deserve it.

## *Hotlines:*

National Sexual Assault Telephone Hotline: 800-656-HOPE (4673)

Online Chat Hotline: visit https://online.rainn.org to chat one-on-one with a trained RAINN support specialist, 24/7

Crisis Text Line: text 741741

## Helpful websites:

https://www.rainn.org/about-national-sexual-assault-telephone-hotline
https://www.nctsn.org/resources/teen-sexual-assault-information-teens
https://www.pausd.org/sites/default/files/pdf-faqs/attachments/teensexualassault_teens_final.pdf
https://cdn.atixa.org/website-media/atixa.org/wp-content/uploads/2015/12/12193513/Teenage-Dating-Violence-Sexual-Assault-Resources.pdf

## Resources for Sexual Health

You might have more questions about when to get tested for STIs, how to get tested, what different types of STIs exist, and how to get treatment for an STI. Maybe you're curious about reproductive health or the different methods of protection and pregnancy prevention. Check out the following information below for more help!

## Hotlines:

Call CDC-INFO 1-800-CDC-INFO (800-232-4636); TTY: 1-888-232-6348

## Helpful websites:

**Sexual Health Information and Resources**
https://www.shorecentre.ca/wp-content/uploads/STI_Comparative_Chart.pdf
https://www.girlshealth.gov/body/sexuality/sti.html
http://www.ashasexualhealth.org/sexual-health/teens-and-young-adults/
http://www.plannedparenthood.org

**How to Start a Conversation about STI Testing**
https://healthfinder.gov/HealthTopics/Category/health-conditions-and-diseases/hiv-and-other-stds/std-testing-conversation-starters

**How to Prevent STIs**
https://www.cdc.gov/std/prevention/lowdown/
https://www.cdc.gov/std/prevention/lowdown/the_lowdown_infographic_poster_30x20.pdf

**Find an STI Testing Location**
https://gettested.cdc.gov/

**Minor Rights to Seeking Treatment for STIs (identified by state)**
> https://www.cdc.gov/hiv/policies/law/states/minors.html

**Resources for Living with an STI**
> http://www.ashasexualhealth.org/stdsstis/herpes/support-groups/ (identified by state)
> https://thestiproject.com/std-support-groups/
> https://wtop.com/health-fitness/2018/06/6-strategies-for-breaking-the-stigma-of-living-with-an-std/

**Sexting Laws:**
> https://cyberbullying.org/sexting-laws

# References

Centers for Disease Control and Prevention. "CDC Fact Sheet: Information for Teens and Young Adults: Staying Healthy and Preventing STDs." August 18, 2021. https://www.cdc.gov/std/life-stages-populations/stdfact-teens.htm#:~:text=How%20are%20STDs%20spread%3F,sex)%20to%20get%20an%20STD

Centers for Disease Control and Prevention. "State Statutes Explicitly Related to Sexually Transmitted Diseases in the United States, 2013." August 5, 2021. https://www.cdc.gov/std/program/final-std-statutesall-states-5june-2014.pdf.

Centers for Disease Control and Prevention. "STD Testing: Information for Parents of Adolescents." August 15, 2021. https://www.cdc.gov/healthyyouth/healthservices/infobriefs/std_testing_information.htm.

Centers for Disease Control and Prevention. "The Lowdown on How to Prevent Sexually Transmitted Diseases." August 15, 2021. https://www.cdc.gov/std/prevention/lowdown/#:~:text=

You%20still%20can%20get%20certain,used%20a%20condom%20every%20time.

GLAAD. "Explore the Spectrum: Guide to Finding Your Ace Community." December 12, 2020. https://www.glaad.org/amp/ace-guide-finding-your-community.

GLAAD. "GLAAD Media Reference Guide." October 18, 2021. https://www.glaad.org/reference/lgbtq.

Healthline. "Sexually Transmitted Diseases: Curable and Uncurable." August 10, 2021. https://www.healthline.com/health/stds-that-cannot-be-cured.

**Leah Aguirre, LCSW,** is a licensed clinical social worker practicing in San Diego, CA. She works primarily with teens and adults who have experienced complex trauma, including childhood abuse, domestic violence, and dating violence, and provides trauma-based treatment including eye movement desensitization and reprocessing (EMDR). Aguirre writes a blog on *Psychology Today*, and has been featured in *Bumble, GQ, The San Diego Union-Tribune*, and in the Reframe and DiveThru apps.

**Geraldine O'Sullivan, LCSW, PPSC,** is a licensed clinical social worker with a pupil personnel services credential in school social work and child welfare and attendance. She currently practices as a school social worker in San Diego County, CA; where she provides mental health counseling services and crisis intervention to teens using therapeutic modalities, including cognitive behavioral therapy (CBT), motivational interviewing, and solution-focused therapy. In 2022, she was awarded High School Social Worker of the Year for San Diego County. O'Sullivan is known for her research on the topic of eustress, which was published in *Social Indicators Research*, and is author of a literature review on the topic of teleworking published by the Southern Area Consortium of Human Services.

## More ⏱ Instant Help Books for Teens
### An Imprint of New Harbinger Publications

**THE RESILIENT TEEN**
10 Key Skills to Bounce Back from Setbacks and Turn Stress into Success

**THE TEEN GIRL'S SURVIVAL GUIDE**
10 Tips for Making Friends, Avoiding Drama, and Coping with Social Stress

**PUT YOUR WORRIES HERE**
A Creative Journal for Teens with Anxiety

**THE SELF-ESTEEM WORKBOOK FOR TEENS, SECOND EDITION**
Activities to Help You Build Confidence and Achieve Your Goals

**SOCIAL ANXIETY RELIEF FOR TEENS**
A Step-by-Step CBT Guide to Feel Confident and Comfortable in Any Situation

**JUST AS YOU ARE**
A Teen's Guide to Self-Acceptance and Lasting Self-Esteem

**newharbingerpublications**
1-800-748-6273 / newharbinger.com

(VISA, MC, AMEX / prices subject to change without notice)
Follow Us

Don't miss out on new books from New Harbinger.
Subscribe to our email list at **newharbinger.com/subscribe**

# Back Cover Material

**be empowered, understand** your **sexuality & build** the **relationships you want**

As a teen girl, you probably have a ton of questions about sex and relationships. For example, what do you do if someone sends you an explicit picture or text, or asks you to send one to them? How do you know if you're straight, gay, or somewhere in-between? What do you do if you find yourself in an uncomfortable situation, or the person you're dating wants to have sex but you're not ready? This book can help you find the answers.

Written by two experts in teen mental health, this go-to guide for teen girls offers practical tools to help you understand and embrace your sexuality, build self-esteem, identify your values and boundaries, and stay safe. Finally, you'll discover what feels right for you, and what to do if something feels wrong. These simple, proven-effective skills will help you handle any situation you may encounter—whether online, via text, or IRL—so you can be empowered and confident!

LEAH AGUIRRE, LCSW, is a licensed clinical social worker in San Diego, CA; and works in private practice with teens and adults who have experienced complex trauma—including childhood abuse, domestic violence, and dating violence.

GERALDINE O'SULLIVAN, LCSW, is a licensed clinical social worker in San Diego County, CA. She currently practices as a school social worker where she provides mental health counseling services and crisis intervention to teens.

www.ingramcontent.com/pod-product-compliance
Lightning Source LLC
Chambersburg PA
CBHW011717220426
43662CB00018B/2402